Complete Italian Workbook for Adult Beginners

Speak Italian in 30 Days!

© **Copyright - All rights reserved.**

The content contained within this book may not be reproduced, duplicated or transmitted without direct written permission from the author or the publisher.

Under no circumstances will any blame or legal responsibility be held against the publisher, or author, for any damages, reparation, or monetary loss due to the information contained within this book, either directly or indirectly.

Legal Notice:

This book is copyright protected. It is only for personal use. You cannot amend, distribute, sell, use, quote or paraphrase any part, or the content within this book, without the consent of the author or publisher.

Disclaimer Notice:

Please note the information contained within this document is for educational and entertainment purposes only. All effort has been executed to present accurate, up to date, reliable, complete information. No warranties of any kind are declared or implied. Readers acknowledge that the author is not engaging in the rendering of legal, financial, medical or professional advice. The content within this book has been derived from various sources. Please consult a licensed professional before attempting any techniques outlined in this book.

By reading this document, the reader agrees that under no circumstances is the author responsible for any losses, direct or indirect, that are incurred as a result of the use of information contained within this document, including, but not limited to, errors, omissions, or inaccuracies.

Table of Contents

Introduction — 1
   A. How to Approach Italian Grammar — 2
   B. Know Your Enemy — 3
   C. Grammar in Every-Day Italian — 4

For Starters — 6
   1. The Alphabet — 6
   2. Pronunciation Pills — 16

Basic Words — 20
   3. Numbers — 20
   Exercises — 30
   Answer Keys — 36
   4. Nouns — 37
   5. Articles — 48
   Exercises — 55
   Answer keys — 65
   6. Time and Date — 66
   Exercises — 74
   Answer keys — 77

Other Words in a Sentence — 78
   7. Adjectives 1 — 79
   Exercises — 86
   Answer Keys — 89
   8. Adjectives 2 — 91
   Exercises — 101
   Answer Keys — 104
   9. Adjectives 3 — 105
   Exercises — 110

Answer Keys	112
10. Pronouns	113
Exercises	117
Answer Keys	122
11. Prepositions and Conjunctions	123
Exercises	129
Answer Keys	132
12. Adverbs	133
Exercises	144
Answer Keys	147
Verbs: Introduction	**148**
13. Verb Groups	148
14. Moods and Tenses	155
Verbs Conjugation 1	**163**
15. Indicativo Presente	164
Exercises	174
Answer keys	178
16. Indicativo Passato Prossimo	179
Exercises	188
Answer Keys	192
Verbs Conjugation 2	**193**
17. Indicativo Imperfetto	193
Exercises	200
Answer Keys	203
18. Indicativo Futuro	204
Exercises	214
Answer Keys	217
Verbs Conjugation 3	**218**
19. Modo Infinito	218
20. Modo Participio	220

Exercises	227
Answer Keys	230
Conclusion	**231**
A: How to consolidate your new knowledge	231
B: Next steps to keep learning Italian	232

~~$29~~ FREE BONUSES

Italian Verbs Cheatsheets
Master Italian Verbs Today!

Scan QR code above to claim your free bonuses!

———————— OR ————————

visit exploretowin.com/italianbonuses

Ready to Sound Like an Italian Native?

Inside these 3 adult beginner-friendly Italian verbs cheatsheets, you'll find:

- ✓ Practical tenses for the most common Italian vocabulary
- ✓ Charts to help you master the conjugation of common Italian verbs
- ✓ Exercises to help you practice conjugating verbs in any tense

Scan QR code above to claim your free bonuses!

———————— OR ————————

visit exploretowin.com/italianbonuses

Introduction

"Grammar is the greatest joy in life, don't you find?"
- Lemony Snicket

Ciao! Welcome to your new Italian workbook! In this book, we're going to unravel the mysteries of Italian grammar and give you the tools to understand how Italian sentences are formulated.

By the end of this book, you should be able to correctly match articles, nouns and adjectives so that they agree in gender and number. You will also learn how to word a sentence and how to use pronouns, prepositions and adverbs. Last but not least, the major goal you will achieve is learning how to conjugate verbs, which is one of the hardcore topics of the Italian language.

If you accept our challenge, you can finish this book and reach an A1/A2 level in 30 days! If you commit to a consistent study schedule, finishing all the lessons within one month is a realistic result and, depending on your pace, it can take less than one hour a day.

If you want to work even harder, and tackle the language from all sides, you can choose to combine your grammar studies with a more practical approach to the language and complement this book with our phrasebook *"Italian Phrasebook for Adult Beginners"* and/or our collection of Italian stories for beginners *"Learn Italian with Short Stories for Adult Beginners"*.

A. How to Approach Italian Grammar

Italian grammar is a dense and complex topic and facing it with the right guide is key to a quick and trouble-free learning journey. Grammatically speaking, Italian is generally considered to be more difficult than English as a language. The reasons are numerous: for example, in Italian there are different sets of rules regarding the gender and number of nouns, and there are more verbal moods and tenses than in English.

With this being said, you will see that, despite the differences, there are a lot of rules, logics, and constructions that are similar to the English. This means that, if you have a solid knowledge of English grammar, you're already one step ahead; in the other case, if you think your English grammar is not in the best place, you can choose to ease your learning journey by dusting off your old remembrances from school. For example, you can find a school workbook for children and see if something still rings a bell.

In our opinion, the best way to learn Italian grammar is a hybrid method that takes from both the old-school and the new-school methods. We believe that the old-school approach to the topics, in terms of when each topic should be covered, is still the best. On the other hand, vast parts of grammar are not very useful in practical terms, as they are just an analytical description of what actually happens in the language. Because of that, we will be discussing the topics in a simple and time-proven order, but we'll skip all the boring parts that require learning lots of information but only grant very little in terms of acquired language skills; in those cases, we'll just present things as they are, without mentioning useless theory and categorizations. We believe that this combination will set the basis for a pleasant-and-steady learning journey.

Moving to the practical side of learning, the best advice we can give is to focus on one topic at a time. Grammar is a complex subject, but each topic is relatively easy if considered on its own. Target one enemy at a time, and you'll see that no part of grammar is too hard for you.

Another fundamental aspect in learning grammar is practice. As the saying goes, practice makes perfect, and a perfect grammar is the ideal goal of every learner of a new language. This book will provide lots of exercises for you to practice with all that you are learning.

This book consists of 20 lessons, each of which targets a specific topic. Ideally, you can finish this book in around 30 days, as most lessons can be finished in a single day (considering an average of less than 1-2 hours of study-time). This includes the time you'll need to practice with the exercises, which will follow every chapter to let you try out your new knowledge.

B. Know Your Enemy

The traditional learning method for Italian grammar starts from what is called "analisi grammaticale", grammar analysis, which is basically about understanding what each word in a sentence is (noun, verb, adjective etc.). The second step, for more advanced learners, should be "analisi logica", logical analysis, which is about understanding what each word in a sentence does (subject, type of verb, direct object etc.). The third and final step, for proficient learners, is the so-called "analisi del periodo", clause analysis, which entails understanding the relations between clauses in a sentence.

This beginners' book will primarily target "analisi grammaticale", which means that we will be mostly focusing on understanding what types of words exist and how they are used. This might not sound like a lot, but we have two major enemies hiding right in here.

Two of the most difficult aspects of Italian grammar are verbs and noun gender. These will be the most difficult topics that we are going to discuss in this book. Noun gender can be tricky, as every word in Italian is either masculine or feminine, and sometimes it is not so easy to tell which is which. As a matter of fact, this can be quite an easy obstacle for new learners to overcome, as newbies have to deal with only a limited selection of vocabulary, but it is a source of hindrance that will always accompany you throughout your studies; even at a proficient level, every time you learn new words you have to remember the gender.

Verbs are another difficult topic, but, unlike noun gender, once you learn how to conjugate verbs you won't have many issues coming up in the future, as the same rules apply to all regular verbs. Nonetheless, this is a difficult subject. A significant part of this book will be about verbs and conjugations, and you will learn all the rules to conjugate regular verbs, as well as the most common irregular ones.

Besides these two topics, the parts with which most people struggle are prepositions and false friends. Prepositions are a real mess, and that's true with most languages. There are some basic rules that can help, but in many cases there's no way to tell which proposition is needed, or what logic is behind the choice of a preposition over another one. Very frequently, you just have to learn prepositions by heart, and through practice and experience, as they don't always follow a clear logic.

"False friends" are Italian words that look like English words but have a different meaning. Some examples can be argomento (topic), educato (well-mannered), morbido (soft) and parente (relative). The reasons why false friends can be tricky are pretty obvious, and we will point our attention to these words as we encounter them. For a more in-depth analysis of false friends, you can check out our book "*Italian Phrasebook for Adult Beginners*", where there's an entire chapter dedicated to these annoying little fellows.

The best practical advice we can give here is simply to arm yourself with patience and keep a lively interest in learning. None of these topics is too difficult, but even the smallest of mountains needs some energy to be climbed. Make sure you never run out of motivation, and you'll learn grammar in no time.

C. Grammar in Every-Day Italian

Every-day Italian, as you could imagine, does not always follow all the proper grammar rules, just like every-day English doesn't always follow its own rules. In particular, there are some principles that, you will notice, are often overlooked in an informal every-day context.

In the past, talking without following all the grammar rules was mostly common among uneducated people, but, nowadays, that type of language has entered common use as a sort of slang, and most educated people follow that trend as well. Some people still support the need of following the old rules, while others suggest that those principles should be lost in the context of an evolving language.

Given the situation, let's see the implications on the practical side. What happens is basically that, if you talk without minding the rules in a formal context, you might make a poor impression and sound uneducated; on the other hand, if your Italian is 100% grammatically correct in an informal environment, you might sound posh or overly sophisticated.

With this being said, the rules officially still stand, and consequently we will teach you a perfect Italian with this book. Once you learn a perfectly correct grammar, you'll be able to knowingly decide if and when you want to overlook some rules.

The grammar rules we have been talking about include the use of *congiuntivo* and *condizionale* moods, the use of some pronouns, and the adoption of some dialectal terms or constructions.

The misuse of pronouns is still considered a mistake, but you should not worry about it too much, as it is not a frequent error among Italian learners. The same goes for the use of dialectal terms. The major situation is about *congiuntivo* and *condizionale*.

These moods are used when describing a hypothetical or unreal situation, typically in an "if → then" form (e.g. "if I could fly, I would never be late for work"). The official rules indicate that the correct grammar would be "if + congiuntivo, then + condizionale" (as we will see in the dedicated chapters); however, frequently people do not conjugate the verbs in the correct way, and instead they use "if + imperfetto, then + imperfetto".

Basically, in informal situations, people tend to use an incorrect tense in those sentences. Also, the overall use of congiuntivo and condizionale moods is often neglected, in all the various constructions that would require them, with people using more common tenses instead.

Besides this situation, it is not uncommon to hear grammar mistakes here and there among Italians speaking their own language.

Moral of the story, in real life there's no such thing as perfect grammar, and it is totally common to make mistakes, even for natives. So don't be hard on yourself when you make a slip, even when you are an expert of the Italian language.

For Starters

In our first two lessons, we want to show you the Italian alphabet and the basic principles of Italian pronunciation. This way, when we get into the depth of the first topics, you'll know how to read the various new words that we encounter.

These two lessons aren't supposed to take you too much time, so don't set your heart on learning each and every piece of information. Go through it, get the general idea, and go on to the next lessons. In the future, when you don't understand a certain pronunciation, you can always come back to these rules that we're going to discuss in a bit.

Another reason why you shouldn't linger on these chapters for too long is that, throughout the book, you will always find a transcription (in an intuitive phonetic spelling) along with the actual Italian spelling, when we present useful phrases.

1. The Alphabet

The current Italian alphabet (l'alfabeto italiano - *laal-phaa-beh-toh ee-taa-leeaa-noh*) consists of 26 letters, 21 of which were part of the original alphabet, while 5 were added later from foreign or ancient languages.

The old Italian alphabet had only 21 letters and consisted of 16 consonants (B, C, D, F, G, H, L, M, N, P, Q, R, S, T, V and Z) and 5 vowels (A, E, I, O and U). The extra five letters that are present in the current version are J, K, W, X and Y.

Learning how to pronounce single letters is very important because, as Italian is a phonetic language, 90% of the overall pronunciation depends on the letter order alone, and the pronunciation is then always consistent across different words.

Let's see how the different letters are pronounced in the various situations. In the following table, you can find the name and pronunciation(s) of each letter, along with a few examples for each pronunciation.

Letter	Letter name	Pronunciation	Examples
A	A - *Ah*	Always like the "a" in far, car, bar	Amore (*aa-moh-reh* - love)
			Arte (*ar-teh* - art)
			Antico (*ahn-tee-ko* - ancient)
B	Bi or b - *Bee or bh*	Always like in English	Bacio (*baa-tchoh* - kiss)
			Buono (*boo-oh-noh* - good)
			Bello (*bel-loh* - nice)
C	Ci or c - *Tchee or kh*	The pronunciation depends on what follows.

C + "i" or "e" makes a tchee/tcheh sound as in cheese or chew.

C + "i" + vowel also makes a tch' sound, and in this case the I is silent.

In all the other cases (C + consonant or H or | Ciao (*tchaaoh* - hello/bye)

Cena (*tcheh-nah* - dinner)

Crosta (*kroh-stah* - crust)

Chiesa (*kee-eh-sah* - church)

Casa (*kaa-sah* - home/house) |

		"a", "o", "u") it is a kh sound as in club or kart.	
D	Di or d - *Dee or dh*	Always like in English	Dente (*den-teh* - tooth) Dieci (*dee-eh-tchee* - ten) Dentista (*den-tee-stah* - dentist)
E	E - *Eh*	This letter can be pronounced as a closed/high vowel, like the "e" in pen, or an open/low vowel, like the "e" in eight. When there's a graphic accent, the closed "e" is spelled "è", while the open "e" is spelled "é". With this being said, this difference in pronunciation varies across regional accents, so don't worry about getting it wrong, as most Italians also get it wrong at times.	E (*éh* - and) È (*èh* - is) Elfo (*èlf-oh* - elf) Europa (*éh-oo-roh-pah* - Europe) Pesca (*pés-kah* - fishing (noun)) Pesca (*pès-kah* - peach) N.B. In this one case, we chose to add tonic accents (see below the table) to the transliteration. This will not be done regularly.

F	Effe or f - *Ef-feh (or fh)*	Always like in English	Forum (*pho-room* - forum)
			Foto (*pho-toh* - photo)
			Forchetta (*phor-ket-tah* - fork)
G	Gi or g - *Jee (or gh)*	Definitely the hardest letter in Italian. The pronunciation depends on what follows	Gatto (*gaat-toh* - cat)
		In most cases, this letter makes the same "gh" sound it makes in English, but not when it's followed by the letter I, E, L or N.	Grotta (*grot-tah* - cave)
			Gioco (*djoh-koh* - game)
			Ghianda (*ghee-aan-dah* - acorn)
			Generale (*djeh-neh-raa-leh* - general)
		G + I or E makes a "dj" sound, as in jeep or gym.	Ghepardo (*gheh-par-doh* - cheetah)
		When it's a G + I + A/O cluster, the I is basically silent, and it only indicates that the G has to be pronounced "dj" and not "gh".	Gnu (*'nyoo* - wildebeest)
			Gnocchi (*'nyok-kee* - gnocchi)
			Gnomo (*'nyo-moh* - gnome)
			Glicine (*glee-tchee-neh* - wisteria)
		✶ G + N and G + L are the most complicated sounds, as they do	Globo (*gloh-boh* - globe)
			Gli (*'yee* - the)

→ not exist in English. In the phonetic alphabet, the G + N sound is spelled 'ɲ; it sounds like the Spanish ñ and resembles the "nee"/"nyo" sound in onion; we'll transliterate the sound as -'nee or 'nyo.

Coniglio (*koh-nee-'yoh* - rabbit)

Foglio (*foh-'yoh* - sheet)

Maglia (*maa-'yah* - t-shirt)

✶ When the combination is within a word, G + L + I make a sound that is spelled ʎ in IPA and is basically a stronger version of the Spanish LL, like in "pollo"; it resembles the English y in year, and we'll transliterate the sound as -'y.

When the G + L combination is at the beginning of a word, it is pronounced like in English, with the only exception of the article "gli"

		('*yee*), and its composite forms.	
H	Acca - *Ak-kah*	In Italian the letter H is always silent and mostly used in combination with C and G as seen before, or in foreign words.	Hotel (*oh-tel* - hotel) Hall (*all* - hall) Ho (*òh* - I have) O (*óh*- or) Hanno (*an-noh* - they have) Anno (*an-noh* - year) Chi (*kee* - who)
I	I - *Ee*	The letter I is always pronounced like the "e" in "me", but sometimes it is practically silent, especially when it's a CI or GI + vowel.	Indicazioni (*een-dee-kaa-tzeeoh-nee* - indications) Imbarco (*eem-bar-koh* - boarding) Già (*geeàh* - already)
J	Gei or I lunga (long I) - *Jay or Ee Loon-gah*	It's pronounced just like the Italian I, except for foreign words.	Juventus (*eeoo-vent-oos* - juventus) Jugoslavia (*eeoo-goh-slah-veeah* - yugoslavia) Jacuzzi (*eeaa-kootz-tzee* - Jacuzzi) Jeep (*djeep* - jeep)

			Jet (*djet* - jet)
			Judo (*djoo-doh* - judo)
K	Cappa - *Kap-pah*	Always like in English	KO (*kaap-paa-òh* - KO)
			Kitsch (*kee-tch* - kitsch)
			Killer (*keel-ler* - killer)
L	Elle or l - *El-leh or lh*	Always like in English	Lungo (*loon-go* - long)
			Luce (*loo-tche* - light)
			Letto (*leht-toh* - bed)
M	Emme or m - *Em-meh or mh*	Always like in English	Mano (*maa-noh* - hand)
			Maschio (*maas-kyo* - male)
			Mulo (*moo-loh* - mule)
N	Enne or n - *En-neh or nh*	Always like in English (except for the "gn" combination)	Nuvola (*noo-voh-lah* - cloud)
			Nuovo (*noo-oh-voh* - new)
			Notte (*not-teh* - night)

O	O - *Oh*	This letter can be pronounced as a closed/high vowel, like the "o" in lost, or an open/low vowel, like the "o" in cold.	Oblò (*oh-blòh* - porthole) Otto (*ot-toh* - eight) Ombra (*om-brah* - shadow)
P	Pi or p - *Pee or p-uh*	Always like in English	Pagare (*paa-gah-reh* - to pay) Pane (*paa-neh* - bread) Partenze (*paar-ten-zeh* - departures)
Q	Q - *Koo*	Normally followed by U, it always has a K sound.	Quaglia (*kwaa-'yah* - quail) Quinto (*kwin-toh* - fifth) Acqua (*aak-kwah* - water)
R	Erre or r - *Er-reh or rh*	The Italian R is always rolled, but not as much as in Spanish.	Rubare (*roo-baa-reh* - to steal) Ricordare (*ree-kor-daa-reh* - to remember) Rompere (*rom-peh-reh* - to break)
S	Esse or s - *Es-seh or suh*	The sound is similar to English, but in some cases it	Sono (*Soh-noh* - I am)

		sounds in-between an S and a Z.	Sonno (*Son-noh* - sleep)
			Sapere (*Saa-peh-reh* - to know)
T	Ti or t - *Tee or tuh*	Always like in British English	Tutto (*toot-toh* - everything)
			Tasse (*taas-seh* - taxes)
			Tuo (*too-oh* - your)
U	U - *Uh*	The letter U is always pronounced like the "oo" in "too".	Uccello (*ootch-tchel-loh* - bird)
			Unicorno (*oo-nee-kor-noh* - unicorn)
			Uno (*oo-noh* - one)
V	Vi or vu or v - *Vee or voo or vh*	Always like in English	Visto (*vees-toh* - visa)
			Vuoto (*voo-oh-toh* - empty)
			Valore (*vaa-loh-reh* - value)
W	Vu doppia or doppiavu (double v) - *Voo dop-peeah or dop-peeaa-voo*	Only foreign words have W's and the pronunciation usually depends on the original language and can be a V sound like in	W.C. (*vee-tchee* - W.C.)
			Wafer (*vaa-fehr* - wafer)
			Watt (*vaat* - watt)
			Wow (*oo-aa-oo* - wow)

		vase or a W sound as in Washington.	Wasabi (*ooaa-saa-bee* - wasabi)
			Web (*ooeb* - web)
X	Ics - *eex*	Always like in English	Xenofobia (*kseh-noh-foh-bee-ah* - xenophobia)
			Xilofono (*ksee-loh-foh-noh* - xylophone)
			Xeno (*kseh-noh* - xenon)
Y	Ipsilon or I greca (greek I) - Ee-psee-lon or ee greh-ka	Always like in English	Yogurt (*yo-goort* - yogurt)
			Yo-yo (*yò-yò* - yo-yo)
			Yeti (*yeh-tee* - yeti)
Z	Zeta or z - *dzeh-ta or zh*	Always pronounced like either "ts" or "dz", with some regional variability between the two.	Pazzo (*pat-tsoh* - mad man)
			Alzare (*al-tsa-reh* - to lift)
			Zizzania (*dzeed-dzaa-nee-ah* - discord)

2. Pronunciation Pills

As we mentioned in the previous lesson, most of the pronunciation directly depends on the letter order. Other than that, the only other factors at play are tonic and phonetic accents, double consonants, and cadence.

Cadence is not something you should worry about, not now at least, as it is something that can be hard even for the most advanced Italian learners. For the moment, let's focus on accents and double consonants.

Double Consonants

Pronouncing Italian double consonants is difficult for most people, and this is especially true for native English speakers, as these sounds are not really present in English.

All consonants can be doubled in Italian (with the only exception of the letter H), while no words that are originally Italian have double vowels. Words with double consonants are numerous and common, so you cannot work around this problem.

The issue with double consonants is that the general idea of "making the sound longer/harder" rarely works, and other techniques must be put into practice. As a matter of fact, only with a few letters you can actually make a longer sound by prolonging the standard sound (this basically works only for the letters F, R and S). For the other 13 consonants, we need a different strategy.

There are two main strategies to teach double consonants to adult learners; let's see these techniques, taking the word "ratto" (rat) for example:

1. The first strategy is to try and make the sound twice. To do this, you should pronounce "ratto" like *raat-toh*. [This is the transliteration we'll be using in this book.]
2. Try and make a pause before the consonant. Pronounce "ratto" like *raa-'-toh*.

You can choose either of the two, whichever works best for you. We'll be using the first one for our transliterations, but you can use the second strategy if you find it to be better in your case.

Accents

In grammar, accents are indicators that a certain syllable in a word has to be pronounced with more intensity; in different words, they indicate what part of a word should be stressed. In Italian, every syllable has at least one vowel, and accents are placed on that vowel.

There are two types of accents:

1. Graphic accents are written accents that are placed on the final letter (always a vowel) of a word.
2. Tonic accents, also known as pitch accents, are normally not written (outside dictionaries) and can be placed on any vowel that is not the last letter of the word. We will not be indicating this accent at all times, as it can get confusing with other accents and because long words can have more than one accent.

In both cases, the accent simply indicates what syllable(s) you have to stress.

Let's see some examples of graphic accents:

Perché (because, why) = *Pehr-kéh*

Però (but, however) = *Peh-ròh*

Sennò (otherwise, if not) = *Sehn-nòh*

Farò (I will do) = *Faa-ròh*

Sometimes these words have a different meaning if written without the accent:

Pero (pear tree) = *Péh-roh*

Senno (good judgement) = *Sèhn-noh*

Faro (lighthouse) = *Fàa-roh*

In this case, the accents we have used for the transliteration are tonic accents, as they're not written. Let's see some other examples:

Ancora (again) = Aan-kòh-ra

Ancora (anchor) = Àan-koh-ra

Ambito (scope, ambit) = Àam-bee-toh

Ambito (longed for, target of desire and ambition) = Aam-bée-toh

As you can see, in Italian there are some homographs that only differ by the tonic accents. In this case, out of context, there's no way to tell which is the intended meaning. This is clearly only true when we read the word, because, if we hear it, the pronunciation will immediately let us know which word it is.

To get around this issue, you can use the audiobook version of this workbook, so that you can directly hear the pronunciation of every single word. This will also help you greatly with your overall pronunciation.

You might have noticed that some accents go from bottom left to top right (like this: é), while others go from bottom right to top left (like: è). The reason for this is that two different accents can go on a letter E (è or é) and O (ò or ó).

The former accent is called a <u>grave accent</u> (accento grave → è, ò), while the latter is called an <u>acute accent</u> (accento acuto → é, ó). A grave accent indicates a closed, high-pitched sound (Mosè - *Moh-sèh* = Moses; Però - *Peh-ròh* = but, however), like the E in "pen" or the O in "lost". An acute accent indicates an open, low-pitched sound (Perché - *Pehr-kéh* = because, why; Roma - *Róh-maa* = Rome), like the E in "Eight" or the O in "cold".

In this case, like in the previous, there can be words that only differ by the type of accent. An example is the word example "pesca":

- Pesca, *Pèhs-kaa* = Peach
- Pesca, *Péhs-kaa* = Fishing (noun)

Don't worry about this too much, though, since these accents vary hugely on a regional basis. This means that, despite a correct version does exist, in different parts of Italy locals use different accents, pretty much randomly.

Take-home message

In these two lessons, we have been focusing on how to pronounce the letters of the alphabet, the double consonants, and the accents.

When studying the alphabet, we suggest grouping all letters in 3 categories: letters that are like in English, letters that are different, and letters that are very different or that have multiple pronunciations depending on what follows/comes before. Give the most attention to this last category; the others won't be much of a problem.

Double consonants and accents have a smaller impact on the overall pronunciation, so these topics should too be considered less important than the pronunciation of tricky letters. Finally, when studying accents, remember that most Italians get some of them wrong, in accordance with regional accents, so do your best to learn the correct version, but don't give it too much importance.

Basic Words

Are you ready to get into the thick of this book? From this chapter on, we will be exploring Italian grammar, starting from the basis. Our long-term goal is to understand how sentences are formulated; we will start by understanding what type of words we can find in a sentence, and how to combine them in Italian.

The next four lessons will target numbers, nouns, articles, time and dates.

With nouns and articles, we'll start learning the first rules about gender and number and understand the very basis of the language. We'll learn how to change gender and number to a regular word, and to some common irregular ones. Then, we'll look into the two types of Italian articles, articoli determinativi and articoli indeterminativi.

With numbers, we'll learn how to count in Italian and how to use ordinal numbers, pieces of information that we'll immediately apply in the chapter dedicated to time and dates.

Each of these lessons will have a practice session at the end. Let's get going!

3. Numbers

Numbers are relatively simple in Italian; with less than two dozen words, you can name pretty much any existing number. In this lesson, we'll talk about cardinal numbers (1,2,3…) and ordinal numbers (1st,2nd, 3rd…). Let's start from zero, quite literally, and see the names for cardinal numbers first:

Cardinal Numbers

Number	Italian	Pronunciation
0	Zero	*Dzeh-roh*
1	Uno*	*Oo-noh*
2	Due	*Doo-eh*
3	Tre	*Treh*
4	Quattro	*Kwaat-troh*
5	Cinque	*Tcheen-kweh*
6	Sei	*Seh-ee*
7	Sette	*Set-teh*
8	Otto	*Ot-toh*
9	Nove	*Noh-veh*
10	Dieci	*Dee-eh-tchee*

*Uno is the only number that can vary in gender and number, meaning that it can be either masculine (uno), feminine (una), or plural (in both genders, "uni" and "une" - quite uncommon).

These are the basic numbers you have to remember; let's now see numbers 11-20. From now on, pay attention to the beginning and ending of words, as you will notice <u>recurrent prefixes and endings</u> that will help you remember how the words are built.

Number	Italian	Pronunciation
11	Undici (un-dici)	*Oon-dee-tchee*
12	Dodici (do-dici)	*Doh-dee-tchee*
13	Tredici (tre-dici)	*Treh-dee-tchee*
14	Quattordici (quattor-dici)	*Kwaat-tohr-dee-tchee*
15	Quindici (quin- dici)	*Kween-dee-tchee*
16	Sedici (Se-dici)	*Seh-dee-tchee*
17	Diciassette (dici-as-sette)	*Dee-tcheeaas-set-teh*
18	Diciotto (Dici-otto)	*Dee-tcheeoht-toh*
19	Diciannove (Dici-an-nove)	*Dee-tcheeaan-noh-veh*
20	Venti (*)	*Vehn-tee*

*There is not a clear logic behind the construction of this word, but at least it kind of sounds like twenty

Most of the following numbers are composite words, and they all follow a basic rule:

If the suffix starts in a vowel (uno, otto), the prefix will lose the final vowel, whereas, when the suffix starts in a consonant (due, tre, quattro, cinque, sei, sette, nove), the prefix will keep the final vowel. This rule does not apply to the numbers 100 and 1000, and their multiples (e.g. centouno, milleuno, duemilauno).

Let's see some examples with numbers 21-30:

Number	Italian	Pronunciation
21	Ventuno (vent-uno)	Vent-oo-noh
22	Ventidue (venti-due)	Ven-tee-doo-eh
23	Ventitré* (venti-tre)	Ven-tee-tréh
24	Ventiquattro (venti-quattro)	Ven-tee-kwaat-troh
25	Venticinque (venti-cinque)	Ven-tee-tcheen-kweh
26	Ventisei (venti-sei)	Ven-tee-seh-ee
27	Ventisette (venti-sette)	Ven-tee-set-teh
28	Ventotto (vent-otto)	Vent-ot-toh
29	Ventinove (venti-nove)	Ven-tee-noh-veh
30	Trenta (Tre-n-ta)	Tren-tah

*because of a general graphic rule of the Italian language, when "tre" is the ending of a composite number, the E becomes É.

Let's now look at all the remaining tens:

Number	Italian	Pronunciation
40	Quaranta (Qua-ran-ta)	Kwaar-aan-tah
50	Cinquanta (cinq-an-ta)	Tcheen-kwaan-tah

60	Sessanta (se-ssan-ta)	*Sehs-saan-tah*
70	Settanta (sett-an-ta)	*Set-taan-tah*
80	Ottanta (ott-an-ta)	*Ot-taan-tah*
90	Novanta (nov-an-ta)	*No-vaan-tah*

The various units in these sets of tens are then formed very simply by using the whole words for both the ten and the unit, but still following the rule about dropping the vowel:

Ten	Prefixes	Examples and Pronunciation
30	Trenta… (2,3,4,5,6,7,9) Trent… (1,8)	Trentadue (*Tren-tah-doo-eh*) Trentuno (*Tren-tah-treh*)
40	Quaranta… (2,3,4,5,6,7,9) Quarant… (1,8)	Quarantatre (*Kwaar-aan-taa-treh*) Quarantotto (*Kwaar-aan-tot-toh*)
50	Cinquanta… (2,3,4,5,6,7,9) Cinquant… (1,8)	Cinquantaquattro (*Tcheen-kwaan-taa-kwaat-troh*) Cinquantuno (*Tcheen-kwaan-too-noh*)
60	Sessanta… (2,3,4,5,6,7,9) Sessant… (1,8)	Sessantacinque (*Sehs-saan-taa-tcheen-kweh*) Sessantotto (*Sehs-saan-tot-toh*)

70	Settanta... (2,3,4,5,6,7,9) Settant... (1,8)	Settantasei (*Set-taan-taa-seh-ee*) Settantuno (*Set-taan-too-noh*)
80	Ottanta... (2,3,4,5,6,7,9) Ottant... (1,8)	Ottantasette (*Ot-taan-taa-set-teh*) Ottantuno (*Ot-taan-too-noh*)
90	Novanta...(2,3,4,5,6,7,9) Novant... (1,8)	Novantanove (*No-vaan-taa-noh-veh*) Novantotto (*No-vaan-tot-toh*)

Let's go on with the hundreds:

Number	Italian	Pronunciation
100	Cento	*Tchen-toh*
200	Duecento (due-cento)	*Doo-eh-tchen-toh*
300	Trecento	*Treh-tchen-toh*
400	Quattrocento	*Kwaat-troh-tchen-toh*
500	Cinquecento	*Tcheen-kweh-tchen-toh*
600	Seicento	*Seh-ee-tchen-toh*
700	Settecento	*Set-teh-tchen-toh*
800	Ottocento	*Ot-toh-tchen-toh*

900	Novecento	*No-veh-tchen-toh*

It's now time for the thousands. With these numbers, keep in mind that mille (one thousand) becomes "mila" in composite words. Let's see what we mean by that:

Number	Italian	Pronunciation
1000	Mille	*Meel-leh*
2000	Duemila (due-mila)	*Doe-eh-mee-lah*
3000	Tremila	*Treh-mee-lah*
4000	Quattromila	*Kwaat-troh-mee-lah*
5000	Cinquemila	*Tcheen-kweh-mee-lah*
6000	Seimila	*Seh-ee-mee-lah*
7000	Settemila	*Set-teh-mee-lah*
8000	Ottomila	*Ot-toh-mee-lah*
9000	Novemila	*No-veh-mee-lah*

The same works with all numbers up to 999,000 (novecentonovantanovemila - *No-veh-tchen-toh-noh-vahn-tah-noh-veh-mee-lah*). Let's just see a few remaining names, and then we're done with cardinal numbers.

Number	Italian	Pronunciation
10-ish	Decina (around ten)	*Deh-tchee-nah*
12	Dozzina (uncommon)	*Dodz-dzee-nah*
1'000'000	Un milione*	*Oon mee-leeoh-neh*
1'000'000'000	Un miliardo	*Oon mee-leeaar-doh*

With big numbers, the words are usually split; for example, the number 1500000 is spelled "un milione e cinquecentomila". ["e" means "and"]

Ordinal Numbers

Before getting to ordinal numbers, we need to take a minute to talk about noun gender, anticipating a topic that will be thoroughly covered in chapter five.

Numbers, like all nouns, do have a gender. Ordinal numbers are rarely used with an article or with other parts of the sentence that would require thinking about noun gender. This means that it's rarely necessary to know this, but they're typically all masculine.

Ordinal numbers are different. With ordinal numbers there's always a someone or a something (or a plurality of people/things) that is first, second, third etc.

Consequently, ordinal numbers need to agree in gender and number with the person/people or thing(s) that they refer to. Fortunately, they all act like regular nouns under this viewpoint. This means that only the final vowel of the word will vary.

As we will see in the future chapters, most Italian nouns follow this rule for gender and number:

	Masculine	Feminine
Singular	-o (e.g. primo)	-a (e.g. prima)
Plural	-i (e.g. primi)	-e (e.g. prime)

For example, if you want to say "the first arrived" this can be:
- Il primo arrivato (masculine singular, e.g. one man)
- La prima arrivata (feminine singular, e.g. one woman)
- I primi arrivati (masculine plural, e.g. a group of men)
- Le prime arrivate (feminine plural, e.g. a group of women)

Like in English, ordinal numbers can also be written in a short version (1st, 2nd, 3rd etc.); in Italian, when the number is masculine, they use a small letter O, like: 1°, 2°, 3° etc., whereas, when the number is feminine, the use a small A, like 1ª, 2ª, 3ª etc. It is not common to use these abbreviations with plurals.

Italians also commonly use latin numbers to indicate ordinal numbers; for example, in a non-Latin context, an Italian would read I, II, III, IV etc. like "primo", "secondo", "terzo", "quarto", etc. This is not very convenient with big numbers, so it is not really used in that case.

Let's see the names for cardinal numbers in Italian, using the masculine singular:

EN/IT	Italian	Pronunciation
1st/1°/I	Primo	*Pree-moh*
2nd/2°/II	Secondo	*Seh-kon-doh*
3rd/3°/III	Terzo	*Tehr-tzoh*

4th/4°/IV	Quarto	*Kwaar-toh*
5th/5°/V	Quinto	*Kween-toh*
6th/6°/VI	Sesto	*Sehs-toh*
7th/7°/VII	Settimo	*Set-tee-moh*
8th/8°/VIII	Ottavo	*Ot-taa-voh*
9th/9°/IX	Nono	*Noh-noh*
10th/10°/X	Decimo	*Deh-tchee-moh*

All the other numbers follow the very simple rule of adding "-esimo" - or esima, esimi, esime, depending on gender and number - to the number name without the final vowel. There is one exception, which are the numbers ending in three (tre); they keep the E (e.g. ventitreesimo, trentatreesimo etc.) Let's see how it works with numbers 11-20:

EN/IT	Italian	Pronunciation
11th/11°	Undicesimo (undic-i-esimo)	*Oon-dee-tcheh-see-moh*
12th/12°	Dodicesimo (dodic-i-esimo)	*Doh-dee-tcheh-see-moh*
13th/13°	Tredicesimo (tredic-i-esimo)	*Treh-dee-theh-see-moh*
14th/14°	Quattordicesimo (quttordic-i-esimo)	*Kwaat-tohr-dee-tcheh-see-moh*
15th/15°	Quindicesimo (quindic-i-esimo)	*Kween-dee-tcheh-see-moh*

16th/16°	Sedicesimo (sedic-i-esimo)	*Seh-dee-tcheh-see-moh*
17th/17°	Diciassettesimo (diciassett-e-esimo)	*Dee-tcheeaas-seht-teh-see-moh*
18th/18°	Diciottesimo (diciott-o-esimo)	*Dee-tcheeoht-teh-see-moh*
19th/19°	Diciannovesimo (diciannov-e-esimo)	*Dee-tchhaan-noh-veh-see-moh*
20th/20°	Ventesimo (vent-i-esimo)	*Vehn-teh-see-moh*

Take-home message

The best strategy to learn numbers is to learn by heart the basic names, and then try to remember the rules to build composite numbers, and the few exceptions.

You can help yourself with videos and other material meant for children to learn Italian numbers. The various songs might look silly and childish, but they're also very effective.

Make your own notes and create a simple scheme for the creation of composite numbers, listing the exceptions as well.

Exercises

1. Name the following numbers in Italian:

3
_____

6
_____

11

1

7

2

4

10

5

8

12

15

13

9

16

20

19

17

18

14
___

2. Name the following numbers in Italian:

113
___

56
___

161
___

1001
___

73
___

2765
___

444
___

10000
___

554
___

82
___

123
___

3. Write the following numbers in figures:

Quindici _____

Uno _____

Sei _____

Diciotto _____

Venti _____

Tre _____

Sette _____

Diciannove _____

Undici _____

Due _____

4. Write the following numbers in figures:

Trentasette _____

Centomila _____

Quarantadue _____

Centosedici _____

Milleuno _____

Sette milioni _____

Diciannovemilaseicentocinquantatré _____

Trentatre _____

Novecento _____

Settantaquattromilanovecentotrentasette _____

5. Order the following cardinal numbers:

quinto, primo, undicesimo, quarto, quattordicesimo, secondo, diciannovesimo, sesto, quindicesimo, nono

1° _____

2° _____

4° _____

5° _____

6° _____

9° _____

11° _____

14° _____

15° _____

19° _____

6. Write the correct cardinal number for each symbol:

3° _____

7ª _____

8° _____

10ª _____

12° _____

13ª _____

16° _____

17ª _____

18° _____

20ª _____

7. Turn the following ordinal numbers into cardinal numbers, then write them in figures:

e.g.   Centocinquantuno   centocinquantun(o)   +   esimo   →
centocinquantunesimo = 151°

Settemila _____ = _____

Cento _____ = _____

Quarantadue _____ = _____

Quattromilacinque _____ = _____

Quattromilacinquecento _____ = _____

Cinquemilacinquecentocinquantacinque
_____ = _____

Novantanove _____ = _____

Milleuno _____ = _____

Tettecentonovantadue _____ = _____

Seimilacinquecentoquaranta<u>tré</u>
_____ = _____

8. Write the correct cardinal number for the ordinal number, minding gender and number (we will use abbreviations for masculine, feminine, singular, and plural: m.s., f.s., m.p. and f.p.):

13 (m.s.) _____

77 (f.p.) _____

814 (m.p) _____

100 (m.p.) _____

112 (f.s.) _____

1013 (f.s.) _____

16 (m.s.) _____

888 (f.p.) _____

1234 (f.s.) _____

200 (m.s.) _____

Answer Keys

1. Tre, Sei, Undici, Uno, Sette, Due, Quattro, Dieci, Cinque, Otto, Dodici, Quindici, Tredici, Nove, Sedici, Venti, Diciannove, Diciassette, Diciotto, Quattordici

2. Centotredici, Cinquantasei, Centosessantuno, Milleuno, Settantatré, Duemilasettecentosessantacinque, Quattrocentoquarantaquattro, Diecimila, Cinquecentocinquantaquattro, Ottantadue, Centoventitré

3. 15, 1, 6, 18, 20, 3, 7, 19, 11, 2

4. 37, 100000, 42, 116, 1001, 7000000, 19653, 33, 900, 74937

5. Primo, Secondo, Quarto, Quinto, Sesto, Nono, Undicesimo, Quattordicesimo, Quindicesimo, Diciannovesimo

6. Terzo, Settima, Ottavo, Decima, Dodicesimo, Tredicesima, Sedicesimo, Diciassettesima, Diciottesimo, Ventesima

7. Settemilesimo (7000°), Centesimo (100°), Quarantaduesimo (42°), Quattromilacinquesimo (4005°), Quattromilacinquecentesimo (4500°), Novantanovesimo (99°), Milleunesimo (1001°), Trecentonovantaduesimo (392°), Seimilacinquecentoquarantatreesimo

8. Tredicesimo, Settantasettesime, Ottocentoquattordicesimi, Centesimi, Centododicesima, Milletredicesima, Sedicesimo, Ottocentoottantottesime, Milleduecentotrentaquattresima, Duecentesimo

4. Nouns

In this chapter, we'll talk about nouns and see how plurals and gender work in Italian. The fact that a word can be singular or plural does not surprise an English speaker, but the fact that words have a gender might feel less natural.

Gender

All words have a gender in Italian, and it's either masculine or feminine (*maschile* or *femminile*). It can often be hard to remember whether a word is masculine or feminine, and there's rarely a strong logic that can help you tell why a specific word has that gender.

With most words, like *ombrello* (umbrella - masculine), *carta* (paper - femminile), *foglio* (sheet of paper - maschile), *sole* (sun - maschile), *luna* (moon - femminile), there is not a clear reason that explains their gender.

On the other hand, when there's a gender difference, in Italian there can be a single word when the English language requires two words. Simple examples can be boy/girl (*ragazzo/ragazza*), son/daughter (*figlio/figlia*), or uncle/aunt (*zio/zia*).

Another side effect of this is that the actual gender of an animal or other being is automatically clear without specifying it, whereas in English it would not. For example, a female cat is *gatta*, a male kid is *bambino*, and a female friend is *amica*.

This also means that you cannot omit gender most of the time; it might not be the best when you don't want to assume gender (of people), or when you want to omit the gender, for example to avoid specifying the sex of someone who you're mentioning.

Number

Before looking at the practical rules for gender and number, which we will see together in a comprehensive table, let's mention something about number. In English, there is basically one single rule for plurals (plus special cases), except for irregular nouns. In Italian, it is a little more complicated than that.

There are 3 sets of rules, 1 for masculine words and 2 for feminine ones (we will see these rules in a short while). Moreover, there are a number of irregular words that can only be learned by heart, for the most part.

Another thing to be noticed is that <u>almost every word is countable in Italian</u>. There's a very limited group of words that don't have a plural (or a singular) version, but, besides these, all words have a plural.

Plural of Italian Words

As we mentioned before, there are 3 sets of rules to make the "plurale" version of a regular noun, but it makes the most sense to study them in 4 different situations. The first two rules that we will see (one for masculine words and one for the feminine) are the most common.

Italian words typically end in -o in the singular, if they're masculine, and in -a, if they're feminine. This does not happen with all nouns, but it does happen with a good share of them. All regular nouns that are masculine thatend in -o, and all feminine words that end in -a, follow a simple rule for the plural:

+	Singolare	Plurale	Examples
Maschile	-o	-i	Amico (*aa-mee-koh*) → Amici (*aa-mee-tchee*) = friend(s) Bacio (*baa-tchoh*) → Baci (*baa-tchee*) = kiss(es) Costo (*cost-oh*) → Costi (*cost-ee*) = cost(s) Dado (*dah-doh*) → Dadi (*dah-dee*) = die/dice Esso (*ehs-soh*) → Essi (*ehs-see*) = it/them Fatto (*faat-toh*) → Fatti (*faat-tee*) = fact(s)

Femminile	-a	-e	Gondola (*gon-doh-lah*) → Gondole (*gon-doh-leh*) = gondola(s) Isola (*ee-sol-ah*) → Isole (*ee-sol-eh*) = island(s) Lama (*lah-mah*) → Lame (*lah-meh*) = blade(s) Mora (*moh-rah*) → More (*moh-reh*) = blackberry(-ies) Nota (*noh-tah*) → Note (*noh-teh*) = note(s) Ora (*oh-rah*) → Ore (*oh-reh*) = hour(s)

Before passing to the second couple of rules, a little anticipation. There are a number of irregular words in Italian, whose plural version you'll have to learn by heart and by habit. These words might trick you and make you believe they're something else.

For example, words like *problema*, *programma* or *clima* end in -a, but they're actually masculine and their plurals end in -i (*problemi*, *programmi* and *climi*).

A second example can be the word *lama* (feminine, =blade), which is regular, and the plural is *lame (laa-meh)*; however, there is a homonym word, lama, that might be mistaken for the first one; this word is masculine, and it means llama; the plural is also lama (same spelling as in the singular), which clearly makes it an irregular noun.

As we were saying, "a good share" of Italian words end in -o when they're masculine and in -a when feminine. This means that there's still a considerable number of words that don't do this (we just saw a few examples). However, most of these remaining words follow a second set of rules.

In fact, most of them end in -e, in the singular. Yes, any "-e"-ending word can reasonably be either feminine plural or singular (masculine or feminine).

Yes, that's not good news, but in the next chapter you'll learn how articles can help you greatly with this.

Words that end in -e follow the usual rule (ending in -i) if they're masculine, but they do the same if they're feminine! Let's look at some examples:

	Singolare	Plurale	Examples
Maschile	-e	-i	il Cane (ka-neh) → i Cani (ka-nee) = dog(s)
			il Padre (pah-dreh) → i Padri (pah-dree) = father(s)
			il Mare (mah-reh) → i Mari (mah-ree) = sea(s)
Femminile	-e	-i	la Prigione (pree-djoh-neh) → le Prigioni (pree-djoh-nee) = prison(s)
			la Madre (mah-dreh) → le Madri (mah-dree) = mother(s)
			la Nave (nah-veh) → le Navi (nah-vee) = ship(s)

Nouns with Particular Plurals

Unfortunately, there are many words in Italian that don't follow these rules that we've just seen. Besides the actual irregular words, there are a number of words that follow specific sets of rules, which we can discuss after dividing these words in 3 groups:

Particular nouns that end in -a:

	Singular	Plural	Examples
Masculine nouns	-a	-i	Poeta → Poeti = Poet(s) Problema → Problemi = Problem(s) Programma → Programmi = Programm(s) Clima → Climi = Climate(s)
Masculine words **ending in -ca or -ga**	-ca OR -ga	-chi OR -ghi	Duca → Duchi = Duke(s) Monarca → Monarchi = Monarch(s) Collega* → Colleghi = m. Colleague(s) Stratega* → Strateghi = m. Strategist(s)
Feminine words **ending in -ca or -ga**	-ca OR -ga	-che OR -ghe	Amica → Amiche = f. Friend(s) Buca → Buche = Hole(s) Collega* → Colleghe = f. Colleague(s) Sega → Seghe = Saw(s)
Feminine words **ending in -cia or -gia**, preceded by a **consonant** (when the accent is not on that syllable).	-cia OR -gia	-ce OR -ge	Arancia → Arance = Orange(s) Doccia → Docce = Shower(s) Pioggia → Piogge = Rain(s) Spiaggia → Spiagge = Beach(es)

Feminine words **ending in -cia or -gia**, preceded by a **vowel** (or a consonant when the accent is on that syllable).	-cia OR -gia	-cie** OR -gie**	Camicia → Camicie = Shirt(s) Socia → Socie = Mate(s)/Partner(s) Farmacia (*Phar-maa-<u>tchèè</u>-ah*) → Farmacie = Pharmacy(ies) Valigia → Valigie = Suitcase Mogia → Mogie = Dispirited Allergia (*Aal-lher-<u>gjèè</u>-ah*) → Allergie = Allergy(ies)
Masculine or femminile nouns **ending in -ista**	-ista	-isti OR -iste	Farmacista → Farmacisti (male) or Farmaciste (female) = Pharmacist(s) Giornalista → Giornalisti (m) or giornaliste (f) = Journalist(s) Attivista → Attivisti (m) or Attiviste (f) = Activist(s)

*Collega and Stratega are two of a dozen words that are identical in the singular but vary at the plural depending on gender.

**These words follow the standard rule for plurals (a → e), but they are still considered irregular; the reason is that normally words don't have an I between a C and E or G and E. This is because, if you remember what we learned in the chapters on pronunciation, -ce- and -ge- make the exact same sound as -cie- and -gie-, so the "I" is superfluous.

Particular nouns that end in -o (all masculine):

	Singular	Plural	Examples
Words ending in -co or -go*	-co OR -go	**-chi** OR **-ghi** OR **-ci** OR **-gi**	Fuoco → Fuochi = Fire(s) Nemico → Nemici = Enemy(ies) Luogo → Luoghi = Place(s) Medico → Medici = Doctor(s)
Words ending in -logo that indicate people	-logo	-logi	Dietologo → Dietologi = Dietologist(s) Psicologo → Psicologi = Psychologist(s) Radiologo → Radiologi = Radiologist(s)
Words ending in -logo that indicate things	-logo	-loghi	Catalogo → Cataloghi = Catalogue(s) Dialogo → Dialoghi = Dialogue(s) Prologo → Prologhi = Prologue(s)
Words ending in -io, when the syllable is not accented	-io	-i	Bacio → Baci = Kiss(es) Calcio → Calci = Kick(s) Figlio → Figli** = Son(s)
Words ending in	-io	-ii	Mormorio (Mohr-moh-rèè-oh) → Mormorii = Murmur(s)

-io, when the syllable is **accented**			Pendio (Pen-<u>dèè</u>-oh) → Pendii = Slope(s) Zio (<u>Dzèè</u>-oh) → Zii** = Uncle(s)

*There is a rule that says that short words, and long words (more than two syllables) where -co/-go is preceded by a consonant, have a plural ending in -chi/ghi; according to the same rule, words longer than two syllables where -co/-go is preceded by a vowel, have a plural ending in -ci/gi. However, there are numerous exemptions, so it might make more sense to just commit the most common nouns to memory and forget about the rule.

**In Italian, when there's a mixed group of men and women, the masculine is always used. Consequently, the word "figli" can indicate either all boys or a mix of boys and girls. This happens with all plural masculine words for groups of people.

Words that are identical in the singular and in the plural:

	Singular	**Plural**	**Examples**
Words ending in an accented vowel	à,è/é,ì, ò/ó,ù	à,è/é,ì, ò/ó,ù	Città → Città = City(ies) Caffè → Caffè = Coffee(s) Lunedì → Lunedì = Monday(s) Casinò → Casinò = Casino(s) Più → Più = Plus(ses)
Abbreviations ending in -o	-o	-o	Auto(mobile) → Auto = Car(s) Foto(grafia) → Foto = Photo(s) Moto(cicletta) → Moto = (motor)bike(s)

Several **feminine words ending in -ie**	-ie	-ie	Carie → Carie = Dental cavity(ies) Serie → Serie = Series Specie → Specie = Species
Several **words ending in -i**, mostly feminine words	-i	-i	Crisi → Crisi = Crisis(crises) Metropoli → Metropoli = Metropolis(es) Tesi → Tesi = Thesis(theses)
All **foreign words** are always kept in the singular, even when used in the plural.			1 jet → 2 jet 1 film → 2 film 1 e-mail → 2 e-mail 1 brioche → 2 brioche 1 goal → 2 goal

Nouns with Irregular Plurals

We have already seen plenty of peculiar cases, and the worst is yet to come. But don't panic: you will see that through practice it's pretty easy to remember the most common of these words. Now we're going to dig into irregular nouns, which we will divide into two groups:

Nouns whose plural is very different from the singular:

Singular	Plural	Meaning
Bue	Buoi	Ox(es)
Dio	Dei	God(s)

| Uomo | Uomini | Man(men) |

As you can see it's just a few words, to which we could add *mio* (plural *miei*) and *tuo* (plural *tuoi*), which are possessive adjectives (my and your, respectively) that we will see in the dedicated chapter.

Besides these words, there are various words that do something very unusual: they change in gender when they change in number. In fact, many Italian words are masculine in the singular and feminine in the plural. Some of these "transgender" words are pretty common:

Singular	**Gender**	**Plural**	**Gender**	**Meaning**
Braccio	m	Braccia	f	Arm(s)
Centinaio	m	Centinaia	f	About a hundred
Ciglio	m	Ciglia	f	Eyelash(es)
Dito	m	Dita	f	Finger(s)
Ginocchio	m	Ginocchia	f	Knee(s)
Labbro	m	Labbra	f	Lip(s)
Lenzuolo	m	Lenzuola	f	Bed sheet(s)
Migliaio	m	Migliaia	f	About a thousand
Mille	m	Mila	f	Thousand(s)
Osso	m	Ossa	f	Bone(s)

Paio	m	Paia	f	Pair(s)
Uovo	m	Uova	f	Egg(s)

Nouns with Multiple Plurals

Finally, there are some nouns that have more than one plural version, which in some cases have meanings that are slightly different. We will just look at some examples (including some words from the previous table):

Singular (gender)	Plural 1 (gender)	Meaning	Plural 2 (gender)	Meaning
Braccio(m)	**Braccia**(f)	Arms (body)	Bracci(m)	Arm(s)
Corno(m)	**Corna**(f)	Horns (animals)	Corni(m)	Horns (horn-shaped rocks or the musical instrument)
Gesto(m)	**Gesti**(m)	Gestures	**Gesta**(f)	Deeds, Achievements
Grido(m)	Gridi(m)	Shouts	Grida(f)	Shouts
Labbro(m)	**Labbra**(f)	Lips	Labbri(m)	Rims
Lenzuolo(m)	**Lenzuola**(f)	Bed sheets	Lenzuoli(m)	Bed sheets
Membro(m)	Membri(m)	Members	Membra(f)	Limbs or Body (by extension)

Muro(m)	**Muri**(m)	Walls (of a house)	**Mura**(f)	Walls (surrounding a castle or fortified area)
Strillo(m)	Strilli(m)	Cries (shouts)	Strilla(f)	Cries (shouts)
Urlo(m)	Urli(m)	Yells	Urla(f)	Yells

The only two common words that you should try to remember, besides the feminine plurals also present in the table previous to this one, are two words in bold.

This chapter will not be followed by a practice section, because it makes much more sense to practice with nouns together with articles. Consequently, the next lesson (articles) will have an exhaustive and comprehensive practice section at the end.

5. Articles

Welcome back to a new lesson! Do you feel tired, depressed and hopeless? If the answer is yes, it means that you did complete the previous lesson!

I know, it was a lot of information all together, and the irregular nouns are just…whatever. But now it's time for the good news! In this chapter, we'll talk about articles. Articles can be very helpful, as they can help you detect the correct gender and number of a word.

Articles are extremely common in Italian, to the point that almost every NOUN in a sentence is usually preceded by one. Also, all articles have to agree in gender and number with the noun they refer to.

This means that, if you correctly identify the gender and number of the article (which is very easy), you will automatically know the gender and number of the noun it refers to, even when you don't know that word.

So, let's talk about articles. There are two separate groups of Italian articles: *articoli determinativi*, or definite articles, and *articoli indeterminativi*, indefinite articles. The former are used before a specific and identified noun (like the English "the"), while the latter are used for general or unidentified nouns (like the English "a/an" or "some").

Definite Articles (Articoli Determinativi)

All articles come in a plural and in a singular version, for each gender. In some cases, there is more than one possible article for a given gender and number, and the choice depends on the spelling of the word that follows (which is also the word it refers to, as the correct word order never separates articles and their nouns).

ARTICLES FOR FEMININE WORDS

We will start with articoli determinativi for feminine words, which follow simpler rules than those for masculine words. The basic rule is:

Singular	Plural	Examples
la	le	La lama (*lah lah-mah*) → Le lame (*leh lah-meh*) = the blade(s) La mora (*moh-rah*) → Le more (*moh-reh*) = the blackberry(-ies) La nota (*noh-tah*) → Le note (*noh-teh*) = the note(s)

ELISION

To understand the second rule properly, we need to spend a minute talking about a separate grammar topic: elision. Elision is when a letter is eliminated, for various reasons, as a grammar practice.

In Italian, when some types of words follow one-another in a sentence, if the first word ends in a vowel and the following one begins also in a vowel, the last vowel of the former word tends to be dropped.

We'll clarify this in a second with some examples. This practice is not always a rule, meaning that it's sometimes optional, but it is practically mandatory to do this with a restricted group of words, with articles being one of them. In different words, <u>when an article is followed by a word that starts in a vowel, the last vowel of the article is dropped</u>. There are exceptions, but very limited.

In these instances, the elision is graphically portrayed with an apostrophe.

Let's get back to the articles for feminine words, and look at some examples of what happens when the word after the article starts in a vowel:

Used before:	Singular	Plural	Examples
words starting in any consonant	la	le	La lama (*lah lah-mah*) → Le lame (*leh lah-meh*) = the blade(s) La mora (*moh-rah*) → Le more (*moh-reh*) = the blackberry(-ies) La nota (*noh-tah*) → Le note (*noh-teh*) = the note(s)
words starting in any vowel	**la → l'**	le	La isola → **L'isola** (*lh ee-sol-ah*) → Le isole (*leh ee-sol-eh*) = the island(s) La ora → **L'ora** (*oh-rah*) → Le ore (*oh-reh*) = the hour(s) La amica → **L'amica** (*ah-mee-kah*) → Le amiche (*ah-mee-keh*) = the (female) friend(s)

ARTICLES FOR MASCULINE WORDS

Masculine articles are a little more complicated, end there are more specific sets of rules:

Used before:	Singular	Plural	Examples
words starting in most consonants	il	i	Il costo (*eel cost-oh*) → I costi (*ee cost-ee*) = the cost(s) Il dado (*dah-doh*) → I dadi (*dah-dee*) = the die/dice Il fatto (*fat-toh*) → I fatti (*fat-tee*) = the fact(s)
words starting in: GN PS PN S + consonant Y Z	lo	gli	Lo gnocco (*loh 'nyok-koh*) → Gli gnocchi (*'yee 'nyok-kee*) = the gnocchi (countable in IT) Lo psichiatra (*psee-kee-ah-trah*) → Gli psichiatri (*psee-kee-ah-tree*) = the psychiatrist(s) Lo pneumatico (*pneh-oo-maht-ee-koh*) → Gli pneumatici (*pneh-oo-maht-ee-tchee*) = the tire(s) Lo scudo (*skoo-doh*) → Gli scudi (*skoo-dee*) = the shield(s) Lo yogurt (*yo-goor-t*) → Gli yogurt (*yo-goor-t*) = the yogurt (countable in IT) Lo zoo (*dz-oh-oh*) → Gli zoo (*dz-oh-oh*) = the zoo(s)

words starting in a vowel (a,e,i,o,u)	lo → l'	gli	L'amico (*lh ah-mee-koh*) → Gli amici (*'yee ah-mee-tchee*) = the friend(s) L'esorcista (*ehs-sohr-tchee-stah*) → Gli esorcisti (*ehs-sohr-tchee-stee*) = the exorcist(s) L'atto (*aht-toh*) → Gli atti (*aht-tee*) = the act(s)

The **take-home message** here is that articoli determinativi are like the English "the", although they are much more common in Italian. With feminine words it's easy, it's always "la", except when there's an elision. With masculine words, the article can be "il" or "lo", depending on the first letters of the noun, and "lo" loses the "o" when the noun starts in a vowel. Remember about these elisions, which produce the article - l' - for both masculine and feminine articles.

Indefinite Articles (Articoli Indeterminativi)

Indefinite articles are used like the English "a" or "some", for things that are being mentioned in general, like "a chair" and not "the chair", things that are not specific or that have not been mentioned before. You're basically just naming the thing, not mentioning a specific object or concept.

ARTICLES FOR FEMININE WORDS

Just like with definite articles, articoli indeterminativi are easier with feminine words:

Used before:	Singular	Plural	Examples
words starting in	una	delle	Una lama (*oo-nah lah-mah*) → Delle lame (*dehl-leh lah-meh*) = a blade/some blades

any consonant			Una mora (*moh-rah*) → Delle more (*moh-reh*) = a blackberry/some blackberries Una nota (*noh-tah*) → Delle note (*noh-teh*) = a note/some notes
words starting in any vowel	**una** → **un'***	**delle**	Un'isola (*oon ee-sol-ah*) → Delle isole (*dehl-leh ee-sol-eh*) = an island/some islands Un'ora (*oh-rah*) → Delle ore (*oh-reh*) = an hour/some hours Un'amica (*ah-mee-kah*) → Delle amiche (*ah-mee-keh*) = a/some (female) friend/friends

*This is an elision; "un" does not exist as a feminine word, so " un' " is a piece of word and consequently needs an apostrophe.

ARTICLES FOR MASCULINE WORDS

Indefinite articles for masculine words follow rules that are very similar to those that we've just seen with articoli determinativi. Here it's a little simpler, with only two articles being involved:

Used before:	Singular	Plural	Examples
Words starting in: GN PS PN S + consonant	**uno**	**degli**	Uno gnocco (*oon-oh 'nyok-koh*) → Degli gnocchi (*deh-'yee 'nyok-kee*) = some gnocchi (countable in IT) Uno psichiatra (*psee-kee-ah-trah*) → Degli psichiatri (*psee-

53

Y Z				*kee-ah-tree*) = a psychiatrist/some psychiatrists
				Uno pneumatico (*pneh-oo-maht-ee-koh*) → Degli pneumatici (*pneh-oo-maht-ee-tchee*) = a tire/some tires
				Uno scudo (*skoo-doh*) → Degli scudi (*skoo-dee*) = a shield/some shields
				Uno yogurt (*yo-goor-t*) → Degli yogurt (*yo-goor-t*) = some yogurt (countable in IT)
				Uno zoo (*dz-oh-oh*) → Degli zoo (*dz-oh-oh*) = a zoo/some zoos
Words starting in a vowel (a,e,i,o,u)		**un***	**degli**	Un amico (*oon ah-mee-koh*) → degli amici (*deh-'yee ah-mee-tchee*) = a friend/some friends
				Un esorcista (*ehs-sohr-tchee-stah*) → Degli esorcisti (*ehs-sohr-tchee-stee*) = an exorcist/some exorcists
				Un atto (*aht-toh*) → degli atti (*aht-tee*) = an act/some acts
Words starting in most consonants		**un**	**dei**	Un costo (*oon cost-oh*) → Dei costi (*day cost-ee*) = a cost/some costs
				Un dado (*dah-doh*) → Dei dadi (*dah-dee*) = a die/some dice
				Un fatto (*fat-toh*) → Dei fatti (*fat-tee*) = a fact/some facts

*What happens here is something that looks like an elision, but, since "un" is a word on its own (masculine), there is no need for an apostrophe (" l' " - from either "lo" or "la" - is just a piece of word, and thus it needs an apostrophe).

The **take-home message** here is that indefinite articles are used like the English "a" or "some". The endings can be in -a or apostrophe for the feminine articles (just like it was with articoli determinativi), or in -o for masculine, plus the article "un".

Notice that "**un astronauta**" is a male astronaut, while "**un'astronauta**" is a female astronaut. The word "astronauta" itself can be either masculine or feminine, so the article is the only way to tell the actual gender, and in this case the difference is only in the apostrophe.

Exercises

Attention: the following exercises might contain words that we have not encountered so far; the meaning of these words is not relevant for the exercises, so we did not provide the translation (to prevent the exercises from becoming "too crowded"). You can always check a dictionary if you want, but we do not advise doing it with exercises 7, 8, 11, and 12, where uncommon words are used.

1. For each noun, cross the correct number and gender:

	Singular Plural	Masculine Feminine
- Amiche		
- Figli	S P	M F
- Alberi	S P	M F
- Mele	S P	M F
- Lingua	S P	M F
- Italiano	S P	M F
- Pasta	S P	M F
- Pizza	S P	M F

- Musica   <u>S</u> <u>P</u>   <u>M</u> <u>F</u>
- Acqua   <u>S</u> <u>P</u>   <u>M</u> <u>F</u>

2. For each noun, cross the correct number and gender:

- Mare   <u>S</u> <u>P</u>   <u>M</u> <u>F</u>
- Padre   <u>S</u> <u>P</u>   <u>M</u> <u>F</u>
- Collega   <u>S</u> <u>P</u>   <u>M</u> <u>F</u>
- Uova   <u>S</u> <u>P</u>   <u>M</u> <u>F</u>
- Opera   <u>S</u> <u>P</u>   <u>M</u> <u>F</u>
- Mano   <u>S</u> <u>P</u>   <u>M</u> <u>F</u>
- Dita   <u>S</u> <u>P</u>   <u>M</u> <u>F</u>
- Dito   <u>S</u> <u>P</u>   <u>M</u> <u>F</u>
- Astronauta   <u>S</u> <u>P</u>   <u>M</u> <u>F</u>
- Prete   <u>S</u> <u>P</u>   <u>M</u> <u>F</u>

3. Write the plural form for each noun

- Amico → _____
- Ragazza → _____
- Sedia → _____
- Libro → _____
- Erba → _____
- Acqua → _____
- Carta → _____
- Soldo → _____
- Ratto → _____
- Ruota → _____

- Palla → _____

4. Write the plural form for each noun

- Mano → _____

- Cane → _____

- Astronauta (Masculine) → _____

- Delfino → _____

- Panda* → _____

- Braccio → _____

- Italiana → _____

- Sole → _____

- Uomo → _____

- Mago → _____

- Moto → _____

*This is a foreign word in Italian

5. Write the singular form for each noun

- Orecchie → _____

- Arie → _____

- Camicie → _____

- Armadi → _____

- Follower → _____

- Lezioni → _____

- Pomodori → _____

- Mamme → _____

- Papà → _____

- Laghi → _____

- Spezie → _____

- Pistacchi → _____

- Piedi → _____

- Denti → _____

- Quinte → _____

- Nonne → _____

6. Find the correct plural for the following singular nouns (more than one answer might be correct):

Barba

A: Barbe

B: Barbi

C: Barbie

Gesto

A: Gesti

B: Gesta

C: Geste

Collega

A: College

B: Colleghe

C: Colleghi

Budget

A: Budgets

B: Budget

C: Budgetti

Dio

A: Dii

B: Dei

C: Dioi

Video

A: Videi

B: Vidi

C: Video

Muro

A: Muri

B: Mura

C: Mure

7. Determine the gender and number of the following words and cross the right alternatives:

- La lucidità   <u>S P</u>   <u>M F</u>

- L'onere   <u>S P</u>   <u>M F</u>

- Il prestigiatore   <u>S P</u>   <u>M F</u>

- Le trombe   <u>S P</u>   <u>M F</u>

- Gli operai   <u>S P</u>   <u>M F</u>

- La collega   <u>S P</u>   <u>M F</u>

- Lo sposo   <u>S P</u>   <u>M F</u>

- L'attività   S P   M F
- Il nibbio   S P   M F
- La generazione   S P   M F

8. Determine the gender and number of the following words and cross the right alternatives:

- Una stregoneria   S P   M F
- Un pazzo   S P   M F
- Dei gerbilli   S P   M F
- Un atleta   S P   M F
- Delle scorpacciate   S P   M F
- Uno stambecco   S P   M F
- Degli pneumatici   S P   M F
- Un'atleta   S P   M F
- Delle congetture   S P   M F
- Una criptovaluta   S P   M F

9. Write the correct definite article (articolo determinativo) for each noun:

- ____ nome
- ____ casa
- ____ sparo
- ____ latte
- ____ banane
- ____ pesci
- ____ bruschetta
- ____ Colosseo
- ____ gatte

10. Write the correct indefinite article (articolo indeterminativo) for each noun:

- ____ toro
- ____ galline
- ____ penna
- ____ pastelli
- ____ telefoni
- ____ radio*
- ____ elefante
- ____ scemo
- ____ xilofono

*This is considered to be an abbreviation

11. Write the correct definite article (articolo determinativo) for each noun:

- Un pentimento → ____ pentimento
- Una bolla → ____ bolla
- Un'attivista → ____ attivista
- Dei criceti → ____ criceti
- Uno sfigmomanometro → ____ sfigmomanometro
- Una derrata → ____ derrata
- Degli scalatori → ____ scalatori
- Un attivista → ____ attivista
- Uno spaventapasseri → ____ spaventapasseri
- Delle scelte → ____ scelte

12. Write the correct indefinite article (articolo indeterminativo) for each noun:

- Il firmamento → ____ firmamento

- Lo scrutinio → ____ scrutinio

- La compagnia → ____ compagnia

- I netturbini → ____ netturbini

- Gli pterodattili → ____ pterodattili

- Le ripercussioni → ____ ripercussioni

- Il cursore → ____ cursore

- Lo zuzzurellone → ____ zuzzurellone

- La crescenza → ____ crescenza

- Gli stolti → ____ stolti

13. Complete the following text with the correct definite article (articolo determinativo). *We don't expect you to understand the text, but you should be able to place the correct article in front of each noun.*

___ migliore amico di Marco è ___ sceriffo che protegge ___ contea. Ogni mattina, pulisce ___ pistola e ___ distintivo e prepare ___ necessario per svolgere ___ sue mansioni. Controlla ___ elenco dei ricercati, sistema ___ scartoffie e si prepara per ___ giornata di lavoro. Quando non lavora, fa ___ volontario; fare ___ vigile del fuoco è sempre stato ___ suo sogno, perché gli piace aiutare ___ persone.

___ esperienze che ha vissuto sono molte, ma ___ esperienza che ha cambiato ___ sua vita è stata salvare ___ bambino che era caduto nel pozzo. ___ pozzo era profondo e scivoloso, e ___ soccorritori non riuscivano a calarsi. ___ amico di Marco è riuscito però a farcela e ha salvato ___ bambino. Così è diventato ___ eroe della città. ___ eroi non sempre hanno ___ superpoteri, ma ___ gesta che compiono non sono da meno.

14. Complete the following text with the correct indefinite article (articolo indeterminativo). *We don't expect you to understand the text, but you should be able to place the correct article in front of each noun.*

_____ giorno, _____ bambina di nome Marta vide _____ farfalla enorme posarsi su _____ amaca nel suo giardino. _____ evento così raro non era da perdere, così Marta cercò di fare _____ foto, ma nell'immagine c'era _____ riflesso. Allora marta prese _____ coperte per fare ombra e le legò a _____ rami. Riuscì così a fare _____ foto perfetta e la mandò subito a _____ amici.

Vedere _____ farfalla e avere _____ occasione per parlare con gli amici sono _____ cose positive. Marta ne fu molto felice. _____ giornata come quella non capita spesso. Decise quindi di festeggiare con _____ cioccolata calda e _____ biscotti.

15. Complete the following text with the correct indefinite or definite article. Remember to ask yourself: "is this a specific thing or is it one in general?"

As we do not expect you to understand the text, we will provide the translation beforehand, so that you can understand which type of article is required. The underlined words, or spaces, correspond to the required articles in the Italian version. As you can see, in English less articles are used, with personal pronouns performing that function in some cases.

EN:

My favorite sport is soccer. It is an exciting and well-known sport in Italy, so people talk about it with () friends and have long conversations. () Soccer games are convenient to watch, because they're easy to add to your schedule. In fact, a soccer game always lasts less than two hours, because there are no () sets or () time-outs. Consequently, the time at which the game ends is always more or less the same.

The team I support is () Juventus. It is the team from Turin, the city where I live. I think that () Juventus is a very strong team. () Companies* as organized as this one are infrequent to see in Italy, and I believe that the strength of a team like () Juventus also depends on this.

The last two years have not been the best, but I hope that the team will get back to winning soon, especially the Champions League cup, which () fans have not seen in years.

*In the Italian text, this corresponds to a particular construction that we have not encountered yet. For the sake of this exercise, just know that the main topic is about football clubs in general.

IT

_____ mio sport preferito è _____ calcio. È _____ sport appassionante e molto conosciuto in Italia, quindi la gente ne parla con _____ amici e fanno lunghe conversazioni. _____ partite di calcio sono comode da vedere perché sono facili da incastrare tra _____ impegni. Infatti, _____ partita dura sempre meno di due ore, perché non ci sono _____ set o _____ time out. Quindi, _____ orario a cui finisce _____ partita è più o meno sempre _____ stesso.

_____ squadra che tifo è _____ Juventus*. È _____ squadra di Torino, _____ città dove abito. Credo che _____ Juventus sia _____ squadra fortissima. _____ società così organizzate non si vedono spesso in Italia, e credo che _____ forza di _____ squadra come _____ Juventus dipenda anche da questo.

_____ ultimi anni non sono stati _____ massimo, ma spero che _____ squadra torni presto a vincere, soprattutto _____ coppa della Champions League, che _____ tifosi non vedono da anni.

*Teams are one of those things that can masculine or feminine without a reason. Juventus is FEMININE, but other teams are masculine and there is no track of reason whatsoever for them to have either of the two possible genders.

Answer keys

1. PF, PM, PM, SF, SF, SM, SF, SF, SF, SF

2. SM, SM, SM or SF, PF, SF, SF, PF, SM, SM or SF, SM

3. Amici, Ragazze, Sedie, Libri, Erbe, Acque, Carte, Soldi, Ratti, Ruote, Palle

4. Mani, Cani, Astronauti, Delfini, Panda, Braccia or Bracci, Italiane, Soli, Uomini, Maghi, Moto

5. Orecchia, Aria, Camicia, Armadio, Follower, Lezione, Pomodoro, Mamma, Papà, Lago, Spezia, Pistacchio, Piede, Dente, Quinta, Nonna

6. A, A and B, B and C, B, B, C, A and B

7. SF, SM, SM, PF, PM, SF, SM, SF, SM, SF

8. SF, SM, PM, SM, PF, SM, PM, SF, PF, SF

9. il, la, lo, il, le, i, la, il, le

10. un, delle, una, dei, dei, una OR delle, un, uno, uno

11. il, la, l', i, lo, la, gli, l', lo, le

12. un, uno, una, dei, degli, delle, un, uno, una, degli

13. Il, lo, la, la, il, il, le. l', le, la. il; il, il, le. Le, l', la, il. Il, i. L', il. l'. Gli, i, le.

14. Un, una, una, un'. Un, una, un. delle, dei. una, degli. una, un', delle. una. una dei.

15. Il, il. uno, gli. Le, gli. una, i OR dei, i OR dei. l', la, lo. La, la. la, la. La, una. Delle, la, una, la. Gli, il, la, la, i.

6. Time and Date

Welcome to your sixth lesson! In this chapter, we will learn how to ask and tell date and time in Italian, and all the related vocabulary.

Hours

Words regarding time are pretty simple in Italian, and they're usually based on a 24-hour clock. The first thing to notice is that the nouns for hours are feminine (la ora → l'ora = the hour - is feminine in Italian - the plural is "le ore"), so all the numbers for the hours will act like feminine words.

Let's look at the table below; here you can see a list of the names for the various hours for the day, in both a 24h clock (mostly used in official contexts) and a 12h clock (common in colloquial settings).

12h	24h	24h vocabulary	12h vocabulary
1 AM	1:00	(la una ->) L'una	L'una di notte L'una del mattino
2 AM	2:00	Le due	Le due di notte Le due del mattino
3 AM	3:00	Le tre	Le tre di notte Le tre del mattino
4 AM	4:00	Le quattro	Le quattro di notte Le quattro del mattino
5 AM	5:00	Le cinque	Le cinque di notte Le cinque del mattino
6 AM	6:00	Le sei	Le sei del mattino

7 AM	7:00	Le sette	Le sette del mattino
8 AM	8:00	Le otto	Le otto del mattino
9 AM	9:00	Le nove	Le nove del mattino
10 AM	10:00	Le dieci	Le dieci del mattino
11 AM	11:00	Le undici	Le undici del mattino
12 AM	12:00	Le dodici	(il) Mezzogiorno
1 PM	13:00	Le tredici	L'una di pomeriggio
2 PM	14:00	Le quattordici	Le due di pomeriggio
3 PM	15:00	Le quindici	Le tre del pomeriggio
4 PM	16:00	Le sedici	Le quattro del pomeriggio
5 PM	17:00	Le diciassette	Le cinque del pomeriggio
6 PM	18:00	Le diciotto	Le sei di sera
7 PM	19:00	Le diciannove	Le sette di sera
8 PM	20:00	Le venti	Le otto di sera
9 PM	21:00	Le ventuno	Le nove di sera

10 PM	22:00	Le ventidue	Le dieci di sera
11 PM	23:00	Le ventitré	Le undici di sera
12 PM	24:00	Le ventiquattro	(la) Mezzanotte

The 24h-clock words are pretty simple; it's mostly just the numbers that we've already seen, except for the fact that with "la una" the number "uno" gets a feminine ending "-a".

The 12h-clock words might need some explanation. The recurrent words that you can see are the names for the times of the day: mattino=*maat-tee-noh*=morning, pomeriggio=*poh-meh-reedj-djoh*=afternoon, sera=*seh-rah*=evening, notte=*not-teh*=night.

"Di" and "del" are prepositions that will be discussed in a specific lesson, for now just know that they both mean "of".

As you can see, the early hours of the day can be considered as either part of the night or of the morning.

The word for morning, il mattino, also has a very similar feminine synonym, la mattina, and consequently all of the above expressions containing "del mattino", can also be formulated using "di mattina" instead.

Mezzogiorno and Mezzanotte are, respectively, Noon and Midnight, and these times of the day are barely ever named using numbers.

Minutes

With minutes, the thing is pretty simple. You just have to add the word "minuti" after the numbers 2-60. The only exception is 1 minute, which is singular and is "un minuto/ 1 minuto". The same happens with seconds, and the words in this case are secondo/secondi. Let's see a few examples:

15 minutes = 15 minuti = *kween-dee-tchee mee-noo-tee*

23 minutes = 23 minuti = *vehn-tee-tréh mee-noo-tee*

1 hour and 1 minute = 1 ora e 1 minuto = un'ora e un minuto* = *oon oh-rah eh oon mee-noo-toh*

3 hours and 33 minutes = 3 ore e 33 minuti = *treh oreh eh trehn-taa-tréh mee-noo-tee*

1 minute and 30 seconds = 1 minuto e 30 secondi = *oon mee-noo-toh eh trehn-tah seh-kon-dee*

*Remember that the number "uno" varies in gender and number, to agree with the noun to which it refers ("ora" and "minuto", in this case).

Telling and Asking the Time

Let's get practical and see how to talk about time in Italian. First, we need to look at a table with some basic vocabulary:

Time Vocabulary			
In punto	O'clock/Precisely	Minuto/i	Minute/s
Mezzanotte	Midnight	Ora/e	Hour/s
Mezzogiorno	Noon/Midday	un Quarto (d'ora)	a quarter (of an hour)
(mezza ora ->) Mezz'ora	Half an hour	Secondi	Second/s

The most common way to ask the time in Italian is: "<u>what hours are they?</u>". The word for "what" is "che", while "are they" is just "sono", as in Italian you can almost always imply the subject, as the verb conjugation is enough to deduce it.

In Italian, the word order does not change depending on whether the sentence is a question or a statement, as we will see later on.

With this being said, the way to ask the time in Italian is:

Che ore sono? = *Keh oh-reh soh-noh?*

The possible answers obviously cover a broader variety of options, but the typical answer would start with "they are…":

Sono le … = *Soh-noh leh …*

The only are midnight, noon, and one o'clock (A.M. or P.M), which are singular; consequently, the answer would be "it's…" → "è…". Let's now see what can follow these dots. You would normally start with the hours, which we already learned to name. For example, if it's 4 P.M, you can say:

Sono le 16 = *Soh-noh leh seh-dee-thcee*

Sono le 4 (del pomeriggio) = *Soh-noh leh kwaat-troh (dehl poh-meh-reedj-djoh)*

There are a few different options regarding what could come after. The simplest scenario is simply adding the minutes:

Sono le 16 e 20* = *Soh-noh leh seh-dee-thcee eh vehn-tee*

Sono le 4 e 20* (del pomeriggio) = *Soh-noh leh kwaat-troh eh vehn-tee (dehl poh-meh-reedj-djoh)*

*The word "minuti" is implied in most situations.

Other options include:

and a quarter = e un quarto = *eh oon kwaar-toh*

and a half = e mezza = *eh medz-dzah*

a quarter to = un quarto alle = *oon kwaar-toh aal-leh*

20 minutes to = venti (minuti) alle = *vehn-tee (mee-noo-tee) aal-leh*

Days, Months and Seasons

With dates, the thing is mostly about vocabulary. The only extra piece of information here is that Italian calendars typically start on Mondays; also, day names are not always capitalized. Let's start by looking at the names for the days:

Days			
Day	Giorno or Dì	Today	Oggi
Monday	Lunedì	Tomorrow	Domani
Tuesday	Martedì	Yesterday	Ieri
Wednesday	Mercoledì	The day after tomorrow	Dopodomani
Thursday	Giovedì	The day before yesterday	L'altro ieri
Friday	Venerdì	Next	Prossimo/a
Saturday	Sabato	Last/Past	Scorso/a
Sunday	Domenica	-	

If you like this sort of things, you might find the etymology of these words quite interesting; they come from roman gods for the most part.

Next on our list are months, which are used just like in English, so all we need to see is the vocab (the names are also similar to the English cognates). We'll also mention the seasons:

Months and Seasons			
Month	Mese	September	Settembre
January	Gennaio	October	Ottobre
February	Febbraio	November	Novembre
March	Marzo	December	Dicembre
April	Aprile	Spring	Primavera
May	Maggio	Summer	Estate
June	Giugno	Fall	Autunno
July	Luglio	Winter	Inverno
August	Agosto	-	

Dates

When it comes to telling the date, there are some differences between Italian and English.

First, the usual order in English is M/D/Y, month, day, year, while in Italian it always is D/M/Y. In addition to that, dates are ordinal numbers in English (2nd, 3rd, 4th of July, June, etc.), while in Italian they are cardinal numbers (*2,3,4 giugno, luglio,* etc.).

The only exception is the first day of the month, which in Italian can be used as a cardinal number as well as an ordinal number (11/1 can be "*il primo di novembre*" or "*l'uno novembre*"). Like most Italian words, dates are usually preceded by an article.

We haven't mentioned the years yet, and that's just because there's not much to say. Italians just spell out the number as it is, and the only thing you have to remember is that you cannot "break it" like in English (for example, the year 2022 is not venti ventidue, but it is duemilaventidue - two thousands and tewnty-two)

Let's see a few examples, where we will change a date into Italian

Date	Digits	Words
9-11-2001	11-9-2001	L'undici (di*) settembre (del*) duemilauno
10-12-1492	12-10-1492	Il dodici ottobre millequattrocentonovantadue
7-14-1789	14-7-1789	Il quattordici luglio millesettecentoottantanove
7-4-1776	4-7-1776	Il quattro luglio millesettecentosettantaquattro
10-29-1929	29-10-1929	Il ventinove ottobre millenovecentoventinove

*These prepositions are usually omitted.

Telling and asking the date

When you want to ask about a date, there are a few options, which also depends on what kind of date you're asking about. A very common question is "what day is (it) today?", but other common questions can be "when... is your birthday?", or similar ones. These are the two examples we will see, and they both translate literally:

"Che giorno è oggi?" = *Keh djohr-noh èh odj-djee?*

"Quando è il tuo compleanno?" = *Kwaan-doh èh eel too-oh kom-pleh-aan-noh?*

The answers to these questions are pretty simple, and you basically just have to tell the date, like we saw in the last table. Depending on context, you might want to just tell the day, or add the month or the year as well. Here are a few possible answers:

"Martedì" = *Maar-teh-dèè*

"il 12" or "Oggi è il 12" = *eel doh-dee-tchee* or *Odj-djee èh eel doh-dee-tchee*

"Oggi è martedì 12 aprile" = *Odj-djee èh maar-teh-dèè doh-dee-tchee aa-pree-leh*

"il 12 ottobre" = *Eel doh-dee-tchee ot-toh-breh*

"Oggi è il 21 ottobre 2015" = *Odj-djee èh eel doh-dee-tchee ot-toh-breh doo-eh-mee-laa-kween-dee-tchee*

As for the second question, if your birthday is, say, on June 6th, you can say:

"Il sei" = "*eel seh-ee*" (if now it's June, you don't need to specify the month)

"Il sei di giugno" = "*eel seh-ee dee djoo-'nyo*"

Exercises

1. Name the following hours of the day:

00:00 → _____

1:23 → L'____ e _____

3:45 → Le ____ e _____

6:59 → Un minuto alle _____

8:00 → Le _____ in punto.

12:00 → _____

13:30 → L'una e _____

13:30 → Le _____ e trenta.

17:18 → Le _____ e _____

19:30 → Le _____ e _____

23:00 → ____ undici ____ _____

23.45 → ____ quarto a _____

2. Fill in the following answers to the question "che ore sono"?

16:15 → Sono ____ quattro e un quarto.

11:20 → Le undici _ venti.

00:00 → É _____ .

01:15 → ____ l'una e un _____ .

20:45 → Quindici _____ nove (di sera).

23:15 → _____ ____ undici e _____ (di sera).

18:00 → _____ ____ _____ (di sera).

6:00 → _____ ____ _____ (del mattino).

3. Convert the following M/D/Y dates into D/M/Y, then write them in italian :

10/15/1991 → ___/___/___ →
_____

12/1/2022 → ___/___/___ →
_____

8/25/1312 → ___/___/___ →
_____

1/30/2001 → ___/___/___ →
_____

3/16/1511 → ___/___/___ →
_____

6/20/1791 → ___/___/___ →
_____

11/17/1999 → __/__/__ →
_____

2/3/2125→ __/__/__ →
_____

4. Fill in the following answers to the question "what day is it today" - "Che giorno è oggi"?

Sept 15th → ___ il quindici ___ settembre

Dec 6th → Il _____ .

Feb 3rd → È il ___ _____ .

July 30th → È ___ _____.

June 5th → Oggi ___ il cinque _____ .

Oct 9th → Oggi ___ ___ nove.

Answer keys

1. Mezzanotte; una, ventitré; tre, quarantacinque; sette; otto; mezzogiorno; trenta OR mezza; diciassette OR cinque, diciotto; diciannove OR sette, trenta OR mezza; Le, in punto; Un, mezzanotte.

2. le; e; mezzanotte; È, quarto; alle; Sono, le, quindici OR un quarto; Sono, le, sei; Sono, le, sei.

3. Quindici ottobre millenovecentonovantuno; uno/primo dicembre duemilaventidue; venticinque agosto milletrecentododici; trenta gennaio duemilauno; sedici marzo millecinquecentoundici; venti giugno millesettecentonovantuno; diciassette novembre millenovecentonovantanove; tre febbreaio duemilacentoventicinque.

4. È; sei; tre, (di) febbraio; il trenta; è, (di) giugno; è, il.

Other Words in a Sentence

In this section, we will spend some time on adjectives, pronouns, prepositions, conjunctions, and adverbs. Each of these topics has its intricacies, but for now we will just focus on the most important parts, for you to gain a first general understanding of how things work with these words.

Our first chapter will be about adjectives; we will see how they are used in general and look at some common descriptive adjectives. Then, we will talk about comparative and superlative adjectives, and the irregular forms. Finally, we will mention the other types of adjectives and we'll linger on possessive adjectives.

This last part will be connected to the first part of the chapter about pronouns, where possessive pronouns will be discussed. We will also explain Italian direct and indirect pronouns.

After that, we will talk about prepositions: we'll look at all the Italian prepositions and discuss the most common uses, then we'll see how they can combine with articles to form the so-called "articulated prepositions". Conjunctions are few and easy, so we are going to give a quick look at them at the end of this chapter.

The last chapter of this section will be about adverbs, and our target will be understanding how they are used and learning the most common ones.

Summarizing, in this chapter we'll see all the other words that can be in a sentence other than nouns and articles - which we already discussed - and verbs, which will require more than one chapter to be analyzed.

After finishing this chapter, you should be able to word a sentence correctly, and to use articles, nouns and adjectives (and all the other sentence-components like adverbs, prepositions and pronouns). We decided to wait and dedicate a separate space for verbs, however, as soon as you finish the first chapters about verbs, you will be able to understand and formulate a large number of simple sentences in Italian!

7. Adjectives 1

Adjectives are words that specify something about the person or thing to which they refer. A simple example can be "a good car" → "una buona macchina". As you might have noticed from this first example, Italian "aggettivi", <u>adjectives, always have to agree in gender and number</u> with their noun.

The second thing to notice is that, whereas in English the adjective normally precedes the noun, in Italian it can either precede it or follow it. There is a general rule, even though in many cases there is not much of a difference between the two options.

Word Order

The basic rule is that the position of the adjective depends on its function. Italian adjectives can be divided either according to the type of information they specify, or according to their function, and this is what mostly determines the position.

Sorting them by function, adjectives can either be "descriptive" (descrittivi) or "restrictive" (restrittivi) - you don't need to remember names or groups, but just the general function. In Italian, "<u>aggettivi descrittivi</u>" (not to be mistaken for English descriptive adjectives) are adjectives that have the function of giving an information about the noun - una piccola casa → a small house (the house looks small).

Restrictive adjectives, or "<u>aggettivi restrittivi</u>", are slightly different, and they indicate a specific characteristic of the noun, thus restricting the possibilities → la casa piccola = the small house (the house has to be small).

This "rule" is rather a general indication, and, in a good half of the cases, choosing either of the two alternatives won't modify the meaning of the sentence. Unfortunately, this also means that in the other cases the order does change the meaning, and will possibly make the sentence sound awkward.

The general indication is to <u>position the adjective AFTER the noun,</u> when the adjective is used to help identify the related thing or person; this is the most frequent case. In the other situations, the two are often interchangeable, except for some specific cases. In these cases, one of the two possible placings is mandatory:

ALWAYS BEFORE THE NOUN

1. Adjectives that are use figuratively

e.g. "an old friend" → "un vecchio amico" (the friend is not necessarily old, the friendship is).

2. Some specific words or expressions (that we'll leave for when you're more proficient in Italian).

ALWAYS AFTER THE NOUN

1. Altered nouns; This topic will be discussed in our "advanced learners" grammar book, and for now just know that Italians can change the endings of nouns with suffixes that take the place of a limited selection of basic adjectives. An example can be "palla" (ball), "pallina" (small ball), "pallona" (big ball), "pallaccia" (bad ball).

2. When the adjective holds a complement; this is also an advanced topic, for now consider it like "adjective + of/with", like "a vase full of roses", or "a face red of rage" ("un vaso pieno di rose", not "un pieno vaso di rose"; "una faccia rossa di rabbia", not "una rossa faccia di rabbia").

3. When the adjective is a verb being used as an adjective; later in this book we will see how the mood "participio" can be used in this way. (This rule has limited exceptions.)

Gender and Number

The rules for gender and number are simple with adjectives, and there are very few irregular words. The basic rule is to change the final vowel, according to the following table:

	Singolare	Plurale	Examples
Maschile	-o	-i	Caro, cari (dear) Alto, alti (tall) Aperto, aperti (open)
Femminile	-a	-e	Cara, care (dear) Alta, alte (tall) Aperta, aperte (open)

IRREGULAR ADJECTIVES

Only four adjectives are considered irregular: bello (nice/good-looking/beautiful), buono (good), grande (big), and santo (holy). The first two adjectives follow similar sets of rules, according to which their feminine versions are pretty much regular, while masculine versions are declined in a way that is similar to what we saw with masculine articles:

BELLO

Cases	Masculine		Feminine	
	Sing.	Plur.	Sing.	Plur.
words starting in most consonants	**Bel**	**Bei**	**Bella**	**Belle**
words starting in: GN PS	**Bello**	**Begli**	**Bella**	**Belle**

PN S + consonant Y Z				
words starting in a vowel (a,e,i,o,u)	Bello → **Bell'**	**Begli**	**Bella** or **bell'**	**Belle**

BUONO

Cases	Masculine		Feminine	
	Sing.	Plur.	Sing.	Plur.
words starting in most consonants	**Buon**	**Buoni**	**Buona**	**Buone**
words starting in: GN PS PN S + consonant Y Z	**Buono**	**Buoni**	**Buona**	**Buone**
words starting in a vowel (a,e,i,o,u)	**Buon**	**Buoni**	**Buona**	**Buone**

Grande and santo follow more independent rules, and they're declined as follows:

GRANDE

Cases	Masculine		Feminine	
	Sing.	Plur.	Sing.	Plur.
words starting in most consonants	**Gran** or **Grande**	**Gran** or **Grandi**	**Gran** or **Grande**	**Grandi**
words starting in: GN PS PN S + consonant Y Z	**Grande**	**Grandi**	**Gran** or **Grande**	**Grandi**
words starting in a vowel (a,e,i,o,u)	**Grande**	**Grandi**	**Gran** or **Grande**	**Grandi**

SANTO

Cases	Masculine		Feminine	
	Sing.	Plur.	Sing.	Plur.
words starting in most consonants	**San**	**Santi**	**Santa**	**Sante**
words starting in "S"	**Santo**	**Santi**	**Santa**	**Sante**
words starting in a vowel (a,e,i,o,u)	**Santo → Sant'**	**Santi**	**Santa**	**Sante**

ATTENTION! All of these irregular forms, for all four adjectives, coexist with the regular versions. The <u>Irregular version is mandatory when the adjective precedes the noun</u>, while <u>the regular form is chosen when the adj. follows the noun</u> to which it refers,

Types of Italian Adjectives

Now that we have covered the basis of structure, let's start analyzing the various types of adjectives, which are usually categorized as follows:
- Aggettivi qualificativi (descriptive adjectives)
- Aggettivi determinativi (all other adjectives):
    - Aggettivi possessivi (possessive adjectives)
    - Aggettivi dimostrativi (demonstrative adjectives)
    - Aggettivi indefiniti (quantitative adjectives)
    - Aggettivi interrogativi (interrogative adjectives)
    - Aggettivi esclamativi (exclamatory adjectives)
    - Aggettivi numerali (numeral adjectives)

For now, we will spend some time on aggettivi qualificativi (the most common type) and learn the basic vocabulary. Then, we will present you with a table of basic vocabulary for all the other types of adjectives, of which we will only mention the function.

Aggettivi Qualificativi (Descriptive Adjectives)

Aggettivi qualificativi, which correspond to the English descriptive adjectives, are one of the most straight-forward types of adjectives, as they simply describe a quality of the related noun, answering the question "how is it?". The English "proper adjectives" follow under this category in Italian.

Some examples of aggettivi qualificativi, other than "a good car" → "una buona auto*", can be "a short man" → "un uomo basso*", "a tall tree" → "un albero alto" or "a small child" → "un/una bambino/a piccolo/a".

*Here, "good" is used figuratively, hence "buona" is placed before "auto".

Remember: the general indication is to always use descriptive articles after the noun to which they refer, unless the case is one of the exceptions that we mentioned when discussing word order.

Let's now look at some vocabulary, and learn the basic adjectives in Italian:

Basic Adjectives			
IT	EN	IT	EN
Allegro	Cheerful	Fresco	Cool (temperature)
Alto	Tall	**Gentile**	Kind
Arrabbiato	Angry	**Grande**	Big
Basso	Short	Grasso	Fat
Bello	Beautiful	Impegnato	Busy
Brutto	Ugly	Intelligente	Smart

Caldo	Hot (temperature)	Magro	Thin
Costoso	Expensive	Maleducato	Rude
Divertente	Funny	**Nuovo**	New
Economico	Cheap	**Piccolo**	Small
Felice	Happy	Stupido	Stupid
Freddo	Cold	**Triste**	Sad

Exercises

1. Couple each noun and adjective using the correct word order, then add the correct articolo indeterminativo (like in the example):

Divertente + Persone = <u>Delle persone divertenti</u>

Brutto + Evento = _____

Triste + Bambina = _____

Nuovo + Amici = _____

Gentile + Uomini = _____

Caldo + Clima = _____

Freddo + Birra = _____

Basso + Donne = _____

Alto + alberi = _____

2. Couple each noun and adjective using the correct word order, then add the correct articolo indeterminativo:

Santo + Edificio = _____

Buono + Evento = _____

Buono + Bambino = _____

Bello + Amica = _____

Bello + Uomini = _____

Grande + Concerto = _____

Bella + Lezione = _____

Santo + Pazienza = _____ (lit. "Holy patience!"→Figurative and idiomatic)

Grande + Sorpresa = _____

3. Complete the table with all the 4 possible suffixes for the correct Italian translation:

Adjective	Mas. Sin.	Fem. Sin.	Mas. Plur.	Fem. Plur
Big				
Small				
Smart				
Stupid				
Hot				
Cold				
New				
Tall				
Short				

4. Translate each couple of noun and adjective, then write them in the correct order and add the correct articolo indeterminativo:

Beautiful + People = _____

Short + girl = _____

Good + Book = _____

Beautiful + Car = _____

Hot + Climate = _____

Big + House = _____

Good + Beer = _____

Funny + young girl = _____

Happy + young boy = _____

Answer Keys

1. Un brutto evento (figurative!), Una bambina triste, Dei nuovi amici (figurative!) Degli uomini gentili, Un clima caldo, Una birra fredda, Delle donne basse, Degli alberi alti.

2. Un edificio santo, Un buon evento (fig.), Un bambino buono, Un'amica bella (lit.→ beautiful friend) or Una bella amica (fig.→nice friend), Dei begli uomini, Un concerto grande (lit. → big location) or Un grande concerto (fig. → great, enjoyable), Una lezione bella (lit. → a lesson that was nice) or Una bella lezione (fig. → a punishment), Santa Pazienza (idiom, no article), Una grande sorpresa (fig.).

3.

Adjective	Mas. Sin.	Fem. Sin.	Mas. Plur.	Fem. Plur
Big	Grande or Gran	Grande or Gran	Grandi	Grandi
Small	Piccolo	Piccola	Piccoli	Piccolo
Smart	Intelligente	Intelligente	Intelligenti	Intelligenti
Stupid	Stupido	Stupida	Stupidi	Stupide
Hot	Caldo	Calda	Caldi	Calde
Cold	Freddo	Fredda	Freddi	Fredde
New	Nuovo	Nuova	Nuovi	Nuove
Tall	Alto	Alta	Alti	Alte
Short	Basso	Bassa	Bassi	Basse

4. Delle persone belle ("belle persone" would mean → good people), Una ragazza bassa, Un buon libro (fig.), Una bella auto OR Un'auto bella, Un clima caldo, Una grande casa OR una casa grande ("gran casa" would mean a → remarkable house), Una birra buona (lit. → that tastes good) OR Una buona birra (fig. → a good/nice beer), Una bambina divertente, Un bambino felice.

8. Adjectives 2

Descriptive adjectives are one of the most common types of adjectives, and, when we think about an adjective, we usually think of a descriptive one. Because of this broad use, and the fact that they indicate a quality, descriptive adjectives can be changed and used to compare different grades of a given quality.

This is why comparative and superlative adjectives exist; we use them to tell which item/person is bigger/better/smarter than another or which is the biggest/best/smartest of them all.

The use in the Italian language is very similar, although there are some differences. Let's see what this is all about!

Comparative and Superlative Adjectives

Italian aggettivi qualificativi can have 3 different levels (*gradi*):

- Positive (*positivi*): when it simply indicates a quality (all of the examples seen so far)
- Comparative (*comparativi*): when the adjective is used to make a comparison. There are 3 types of aggettivi comparativi:
    - Comparativo di maggioranza (= majority) → e.g. more beautiful
    - Comparativo di minoranza (= minority) → e.g. less beautiful
    - Comparativo di uguaglianza (= equality) → e.g. equally beautiful
- Superlative (*superlativi*): when the quality is expressed to its maximum. There are 2 types of aggettivi superlativi:
    - Superlativo relativo (= relative) → e.g. the most beautiful (of the group)
    - Superlativo assoluto (= absolute) → e.g. very beautiful

COMPARATIVE ADJECTIVES

The basic structure of comparative adjectives applies to all 3 types of aggettivi comparativi, and it calls for an adverb before the adjective and a preposition or adverb before the second term of comparison.

These prepositions and adverbs are different and specific to the single type of aggettivo comparativo. Let's see the different cases, taking as example a comparison in height between Marco and Luca. The word for "tall" is "alto" and the word for "is" is "è".

Comparativo di maggioranza (Marco is taller than Luca)

Before the adjective	Before the second term	Example
più*	**di**	Marco è **più** alto **di** Luca.

* The adverb "più" means "more"

Comparativo di minoranza (Marco is less tall than Luca)

Before the adjective	Before the second term	Example
meno*	**di**	Marco è **meno** alto **di** Luca.

* The adverb "meno" means "less"

Comparativo di uguaglianza (Marco is as tall as Luca)

Before the adjective*	Before the second term	Example

così** OR tanto***	quanto	Marco è alto **quanto** Luca.
		Marco è **tanto** alto **quanto** Luca
		Marco è alto **tanto quanto** Luca.

*With comparativo di uguaglianza, the adverb before the first term is usually omitted, and, if not, it can be either put before ofir after the noun.

** The adverb "così" means "so" or "as"

*** The adverb "tanto" means "much" or "as much"

SUPERLATIVE ADJECTIVES

The two types of Italian superlative adjectives are rather different:

Superlativo relativo is used when the indicated quality is at its maximum, or minimum, in relation to a given group. Since they can indicate either an exceptionally good or an exceptionally bad expression of that quality, there are two types of superlativo relativo.

The superlativo relativo di maggioranza (= majority) is a maximum: Maria is the most beautiful. Maria is the most beautiful - e.g. - girl in the room.

The superlativo relativo di minoranza (=minority) in a minimum: Maria is the least beautiful. Maria is the least beautiful - e.g. - girl in the room.

Superlativo assoluto is used when the considered quality is at its maximum, in general and without comparisons. (Maria is very beautiful.)

SUPERLATIVO RELATIVO

Superlativo relativo di maggioranza:

Before the adjective	Before the second term	Example
il/lo/la/i/gli/le + più*	di/tra/fra OR no second term**	Maria è **la più** bella. Maria e Paola sono **le più** belle **tra** le mie amiche. (*among my friends*) Luca e Paolo sono **i più** belli **di** noi. (of us)

* "più" does not change to agree in gender and number with other words, unlike the article that precedes it.

** when the group among which the quality is at its max is not specified.

Superlativo relativo di minoranza:

Before the adjective	Before the second term	Example
il/lo/la/i/gli/le + meno*	di/tra/fra OR no second term**	Maria è **la meno** bella. Maria e Paola sono **le meno** belle **tra** le mie amiche. (*among my friends*) Luca e Paolo sono **i meno** belli **di** noi. (of us)

* "meno" does not change to agree in gender and number with other words, unlike the article that precedes it.

** when the group among which the quality is at its max is not specified.

SUPERLATIVO ASSOLUTO

Superlativo assoluto is used when you want to say that something is VERY big/small/red/good etc. In Italian, there are 4 different ways to form a superlativo assoluto; two of these are used in a way that is similar to the English, while the other two are something quite different:

1. By using the suffix **-issimo** (or -issima/e/i)
2. By adding an adverb (like **molto**, decisamente, assai, estremamente...)
3. By adding a prefix (like **super-**, iper-, ultra-, mega-, arci, stra-...)
4. By **doubling up** the adjective (e.g. bello bello, alto alto, grande grande...)

The first two options are definitely the most common, but the other two are not unusual either.

Let's look at few examples, with all the 4 possible alternatives for the adjective:

EN	Luca is very intelligent.
+ suffix	Luca è intelligent**issimo***.
+ adverb	Luca è **molto** intelligente. (very) Luca è **estremamente** intelligente. (extremely) Luca è **decisamente** intelligente. (definitely) Luca è **assai** intelligente. (very)

+ prefix	Luca è **super**-intelligente.**
	Luca è **iper**-intelligente.
	Luca è **ultra**-intelligente.
	Luca è **mega**-intelligente.
x2	Luca è **intelligente intelligente**.***

* As usual, the last vowel is dropped when adding a suffix.

** In rare cases the "-" can be omitted and the words can be joined up.

*** Although correct, this example is not very realistic, as this solution is especially common with short adjectives.

EN	The house is very big.
+ **suffix**	La casa è grand**issima**.
+ **adverb**	La casa è **molto** grande.
	La casa è **estremamente** grande.
	La casa è **decisamente** grande.
+ **prefix**	La casa è **super**-grande
	La casa è **ultra**-grande.
x2	La casa è **grande grande***.

*This is a realistic example, meaning that it's something you can actually hear people say. This is because "grande" is a short adjective, unlike "intelligente".

EN	Italy is a very beautiful country.
+ suffix	L'Italia è un bell**issimo** paese.
+ adverb	L'Italia è un paese **molto** bello.* L'Italia è un paese **decisamente** bello.*
+ prefix	L'Italia è un paese **super**-bello. L'Italia è un paese **stra**-bello.
x2	L'Italia è un paese **bello bello**.

IRREGULAR COMPARATIVE AND SUPERLATIVE ADJECTIVES

There are a few adjectives that form comparative and superlative versions in an irregular way. First of all, there's a small group of words, mostly uncommon adjectives, that can have a superlative version ending in -errimo, along with the -issimo version. Beside these, which were barely worth mentioning, there are 3 very basic adjectives that are irregular:

BUONO

We have already seen that the Italian for "good" is an irregular adjective when it comes to declination in gender and number.

POSITIVO*: **Buono** = Good

COMPARATIVO: **Migliore** or **Meglio** or **Più buono/a/i/e** = Better

SUPERLATIVO RELATIVO: **Il/la/i/le migliore/i****   or

   Il/la/i/le più buon/o/i/a/e = The best

SUPERLATIVO ASSOLUTO: **Ottimo/a/e/i** or regular versions = Excellent, Great

* "Aggettivo positivo" is the name for the simple form of the adjective

** This word does not change with gender, only with number

Are the different versions interchangeable? Can I use either the regular or irregular version at all times? Unfortunately, no. Let's explain why:

In Italian, Buono has a more limited selection of possible meanings than the English "good". It literally only has two meanings, and it either means "morally good" or "that has a good taste or smell". All the other uses are considered to be figurative uses of the word. Nonetheless, this practice is extremely common, especially when the literal meaning would be "worthy", as in: "a good car", "a good employee", "a good friend" etc. These things/people are not (necessarily) morally good, nor do they taste or smell good; they're worthy.

Well, whenever the adjective "buono" is used figuratively, the irregular version is mandatory. On the contrary, when it's being used literally (morally good, or that tastes/smells good) the regular version is to be chosen. With superlativo assoluto there's a little less difference than with the others, but the rule can still stand.

Let's see a couple of critical examples:

Questa pizza è migliore/meglio di quella. → This pizza is better than that (pizza).

Questa pizza è più buona di quella. → This pizza tastes better than that (pizza).

As you can see, the sole use of the regular version automatically makes it clear that we're talking about taste, as the literal meaning must be being used.

Luca è la persona migliore che conosco. → Luca is the best person I know.

Luca è la persona più buona che conosco. → Luca is the kindest/most wholesome person I know.

Again, the choice of the regular VS irregular version is enough to change the meaning, as it implies which of the two possible meanings (figurative or literal) is being used.

CATTIVO

Cattivo is the Italian for "bad" or "evil", and it is used exactly like buono. There are both regular and irregular comparative and superlative forms, and the irregular one is mandatory when the word is used figuratively (which means in all cases except for when it means evil/morally bad or that tastes/smells bad).

POSITIVO: **Cattivo** = Bad, Evil, Despicable

COMPARATIVO: **Peggiore** or **Peggio** or **Più cattivo/a/i/e** = Worse

SUPERLATIVO RELATIVO: **Il/la/i/le peggiore/i*** or

  Il/la/i/le più cattivo/i/a/e = The worst

SUPERLATIVO ASSOLUTO: **Pessimo/a/e/i** or regular versions = Terrible, Awful

* This word does not change with gender, only with number

Examples:

Questa pizza è peggiore/peggio di quella. → This pizza is worse than that (pizza).

Questa pizza è più cattiva di quella. → This pizza tastes worse than that (pizza).

Luca è la persona peggiore che conosco. → Luca is the worst person I know.

Luca è la persona più cattiva che conosco. → Luca is the evilest/meanest/most despicable person I know.

GRANDE

This is also an old friend, if you remember. The rules for its comparative and superlative forms are similar to what we've just seen with buono and cattivo, except that here it falls in line with English a little more:

POSITIVO: **Grande** = Big, Great

COMPARATIVO: **Maggiore** or **Più grande/i** = Bigger or Elder or Greater

SUPERLATIVO RELATIVO: **Il/la/i/le maggiore/i***   or

   Il/la/i/le più grande/i = The biggest or The eldest or The greatest

SUPERLATIVO ASSOLUTO: **Massimo/a/e/i** or regular forms = Biggest, Best

* This word does not change with gender, only with number

Here too, the alternatives are not always interchangeable. When the noun is used literally (physically big) it is mandatory to use one of the regular versions, while, when you use the word figuratively (elder brother, greater force, bigger impact etc…), the different versions are interchangable.

Let's see a quick example:

Marco è il fratello maggiore. → Marco is the eldest brother.

Marco è il fratello più grande. → Marco is the eldest brother.

Questa casa è più grande. → This house is bigger.

Questa casa è maggiore. → *This does not make sense in Italian.*

Mind that "maggiore" can mean both elder brother ("un" fratello maggiore) or eldest brother (il maggiore dei fratelli), as the comparativo and superlativo relativo forms are identical except for the article and general construction.

PICCOLO

This word means "small", it is a perfect antonym for "grande" and it follows the exact same rules, so we are just going to mention the irregular forms:

POSITIVO: **Piccolo** = Small, Tiny

COMPARATIVO: **Minore** or **Più piccolo/a/i/e** = Smaller or Younger

SUPERLATIVO RELATIVO: **Il/la/i/le minore/i***   or

  Il/la/i/le più piccolo/a/i/e = The smallest or The youngest

SUPERLATIVO ASSOLUTO: **Minimo/a/e/i** or regular forms = Smallest, Minimal, Least

* This word does not change with gender, only with number

Examples:

Marco è il fratello minore. → Marco is the youngest brother.

Marco è il fratello più piccolo. → Marco is the youngest brother.

Questa casa è più piccola. → This house is smaller.

Questa casa è minore. → *This does not make sense in Italian.*

Exercises

1. Complete the following sentences using the <u>comparativo di maggioranza</u> and the <u>superlativo relativo</u> forms of the given adjective:

[alto] Marco è _____ di Luca. Marco è _____.

[divertente] Maria è _____ di Lucia. Maria è _____.

[buono] Questo calzone è _____ di quello. Questo calzone è _____.

[buono] Queste auto sono _____ di quelle. Queste auto sono _____.

[gentile] Marco è _____ Luca. Marco è _____.

[basso] Maria è _____ Lucia. Maria è _____.

[freddo] Questa casa è _____ quella. Questa casa è _____.

[piccolo] Marco è _____ Luca. Marco è _____.

2. Complete the following sentences using the <u>comparativo di minoranza</u> and the <u>superlativo relativo</u> forms of the given adjective:

[triste] Marco è _____ Luca. Marco è _____.

[felice] Marco è _____ Luca. Marco è _____.

[grande] Marco è _____ Luca. Marco è _____.

[caldo] Questa birra è _____ quella. Questa è _____.

[nuovo] Questo libro è _____ quello. Questo è _____.

3. Complete the following sentences using the <u>comparativo di uguaglianza</u> form of the given adjective:

[divertente] Marco è _____ Luca.

[alto] Marco e Luca sono _____ Paolo e Giorgio.

[felice] Questa bambina è _____ quella.

[freddo] Questa pasta è _____ quella.

4. Complete the following sentences using one of the superlativo assoluto forms of the given adjective:

[alto] Marco è _____issimo .

[divertente] Marco è molto _____ .

[buono] Questo calzone è super-_____ .

[felice] Questa bambina è _____issima .

[freddo] Questa pasta è _____issima .

[felice] Marco e Paolo sono super-_____ .

[stupido] Marco è _____issimo.

[caldo] Questa birra è molto _____ .

Answer Keys

1. più alto, il più alto; più divertente, la più divertente; più buono (lit. → that tastes better) OR migliore (fig. → that is better), il più buono OR il migliore (accordingly); migliori (fig.), le migliori; più gentile di, il più gentile; più bassa di, la più bassa; più fredda di, la più bella; più piccolo di OR minore di, il più piccolo OR il minore.

2. meno triste di, il meno triste; meno felice di, il meno felice; meno grande di OR minore di, il meno grande OR il minore; meno calda di, la meno calda; meno nuovo di, il meno nuovo.

3. (tanto) divertente quanto, (tanto) alti quanto, (tanto) felice quanto, (tanto) fredda quanto.

4. alt, divertente, buono, felic, fredd, felici, stupid, calda.

9. Adjectives 3

In this chapter, we will see all the other types of adjectives, which Italians group under the umbrella name of "aggettivi determinativi", as opposed to "aggettivi qualificativi". In particular, we'll spend a little more time on possessive adjectives, which are a basic part of any language.

Aggettivi determinativi

Aggettivi determinativi include all the other existing adjectives, and they are mostly adjectives that specify things that are not really qualities. Let's look at the various kinds, and name the most common adjectives for each category.

AGGETTIVI DIMOSTRATIVI (DEMONSTRATIVE ADJECTIVES)

These adjectives are like "this" and "that" in English. There are 3 main demonstrative adjectives in Italian, one of which is almost in disuse:

- **Questo**/a/i/e = this/these → near the speaker
- **Quel*/Quello**/a/i/e = that/those → near the listener
- Codesto/a/i/e = this/that/these/those → in-between the speaker and listener

*Quel and Quello work like "il" and "lo" or "bel" and "bello"

AGGETTIVI INDEFINITI (QUANTITATIVE ADJECTIVES)

These adjectives indicate an indefinite quantity. This time we need to cover a larger number of words, so we are going to use a table:

IT	EN	IT	EN
Meno*	Less	**Più***	More
Molto	Very	**Qualche***	Some

Nessuno	No/None/No one	Qualunque*	Every/Any
Ogni*	Each/Every	Tanto	A lot
Ognuno	Each one	Troppo	Too much
Poco	Few/Little	Tutto	All

*These ones do not vary in gender and number

AGGETTIVI INTERROGATIVI (INTERROGATIVE ADJECTIVES)

Interrogative adjectives are used to ask questions; the most common are:

- **Che** = what
- **Qual*/quale** = which/what
- **Quanto** = how (much, long, big…)

*This version without the final "E" is most commonly used in the expression "qual è …" → "which is…?".

Let's see some examples:

Che ore sono? = What hours are they? → What time is it? [*keh oh-reh soh-noh?*]

Quale libro è il migliore? = Which book is the best? [*kwaa-leh lee-broh èh eel mee-'yoh-reh?*]

Quanta pasta vuoi? = How much pasta do you want? [*kwaan-tah paas-tah voo-oh-ee?*]

As you can see, in Italian the word order does not change with questions, and you either know that it is a question because of the question mark (in reading) or the intonation (in listening and speaking). The change in intonation is just like the one we use in colloquial English, e.g. "You lost it?", "You saw him?", "He's a cop?"etc.

In this specific case, the presence of an interrogative adjective is also clarifying.

AGGETTIVI ESCLAMATIVI (EXCLAMATORY ADJECTIVES)

These adjectives simply represent a different use of aggettivi interrogativi, in an exclamatory connotation.

- **Che** = what
- **Quale** = which/what
- **Quanto** = how (much, long, big...)

Let's see some examples:

Che idiota! = What idiot! → What an idiot! [*keh ee-deeoh-tah!*]

Quale onore!* = What honor! → What an honor! [*kwaa-leh oh-noh-reh!*]

Quanto spreco! = How much waste! [*kwaan-toh spreh-koh!*]

*When "quale" is used in an exclamatory connotation, it doesn't really mean "which"; it's rather just a fancier or more artistic way to say "che.." -e,g.- "onore!", which is also correct and commonly used.

AGGETTIVI NUMERALI (NUMERAL ADJECTIVES)

Aggettivi numerali are simply cardinal or ordinal numbers used as an adjective. There are no criticalities here, except that you have to remember that "uno" has to agree in gender and number to the noun it refers to.

Let's look at a few examples:

Io ho quarant'anni. = I have forty years. → I'm forty years old.

Io ho una mela. = I have an/one apple.

Oggi è il terzo giorno di vacanza. = Today is the third day of vacation.

Beside these, there are just a bunch more words that, for now, we just need to mention. Let's look at this short table:

IT	EN
Doppio	Double
Entrambi/e*	Both of the two
Mezzo	Half
Triplo	Triple

*Only plural forms exist

AGGETTIVI POSSESSIVI (POSSESSIVE ADJECTIVES)

Aggettivi possessivi are a basic element of any language, both in academic learning and in absorbing the language as a child. The best way to present them is with a simple table:

IT	EN
Mio	My
Tuo	Your
Suo	His

Suo	Her
Suo	Its
Nostro	Our
Vostro	Your
Loro	Their

Mind that all of these adjectives need to agree in gender and number with the noun they refer to, but not all of them form regular plurals and feminine versions:

Mas. Sin.	Fem. Sin.	Mas. Plur.	Fem. Plur
Mio	Mia	**Miei**	Mie
Tuo	Tua	**Tuoi**	Tue
Suo	Sua	**Suoi**	Sue
Nostro	Nostra	Nostri	Nostre
Vostro	Vostra	Vostri	Vostre
Loro	**Loro**	**Loro**	**Loro**

Exercises

1. Complete the following lines and add the correct articolo determinativo and possessive adjective (like in the example).

[my] La _____ mia _____ mela.

[your - singular] _____ _____ amiche.

[her] _____ _____ cani.

[their] _____ _____ libri.

[our] _____ _____ auto.

[my] _____ _____ alberi.

[your - singular] _____ _____ gatti.

[their] _____ _____ casa.

[your - plural] _____ _____ pizze.

[my] _____ _____ mano.

2. Complete the following lines and add the correct articolo determinativo and possessive adjective.

[our] _____ _____ passaporti.

[my] _____ _____ amici.

[her] _____ _____ uovo.

[their] _____ _____ braccia.

[your - plural] _____ _____ parenti.

[his] _____ _____ psichiatra.

[my] _____ _____ yogurt.

[its] _____ _____ uova.

[your - singular] _____ _____ cane.

3. Translate the following lines:

A: How many books? → A: _____ ?
B: Two. → B: _____ .

C: What time is it? → C: _____ ?
D: It's 6 PM. → D: _____ .

E: Which dog? → E: _____ ?
F: This dog. → F: _____ .

G: How much is this book? → G: _____ ?
H: Five euro. → H: _____ euro.

I: What an honor! → I: _____ !

J: What a goal! → J: _____ goal!

K: How stupid! → K: _____ !

L: How much ignorance! → [ignoranza] → L: _____ !

Answer Keys

1. Le tue; I suoi; I loro; La nostra OR Le nostre; I miei; I tuoi; La loro; Le vostre; La mia.

2. I nostri; I miei; Il suo; Le loro; I vostri; Il suo OR La sua; Il mio OR I miei; Le sue; Il tuo.

3.
    A. Quanti libri
    B. Due
    C. Che ore sono
    D. Sono le sei del pomeriggio OR Sono le diciotto OR Sono le sei di sera
    E. Quale cane
    F. Questo cane
    G. Quanto costa questo libro
    H. Cinque
    I. Che onore OR Quale onore
    J. Che
    K. Che stupido
    L. Quanta ignoranza

10. Pronouns

Pronouns are words that can take the place of other nouns; this usually happens when it's useless specifying the noun or to avoid repetition.

For the moment, we will see 2 different types of pronouns: pronomi personali (personal pronouns) and pronomi dimostrativi (demonstrative pronouns).

Pronomi Personali (Personal Pronouns)

There are 2 different types of personal pronouns:

- **Pronomi personali soggetto** are used when the replaced <u>noun is the subject</u> of the sentence.
- **Pronomi personali complemento** are used when the replaced <u>noun is a complement</u> in the sentence. These pronouns can be grouped in 2 categories:
    - **Pronomi diretti** are used when the pronoun is a <u>direct object</u>.
    - **Pronomi indiretti** are used for "complemento di termine", a complement that <u>specifies the receiver of an action.</u>

PRONOMI PERSONALI SOGGETTO

These are the simplest kind of personal pronouns, as you can see from the following table:

IT	EN
Io	My
Tu	Your
Lui, Egli	His

Lei, Ella	Her
Esso, Essa*	Its
Noi	Our
Voi	Your
Loro, Essi, Esse*	Their

*Esso and Essa are used for inanimate masculine and feminine objects. Essi and Esse can also be used for animate beings.

PRONOMI PERSONALI COMPLEMENTO

Pronouns that are used as a complement are a little more complicated. First of all, all pronouns of both categories (direct and indirect) exist in 2 separate versions, which are usually named "forma forte" (strong form) and "forma debole" (weak form), although the names simply refer to the pronunciations, which is more high-pitched for the former group, as the spelling can suggest.

The adjectives in "forma forte" always come after the verb, while adjectives in forma debole are used just before the verb, or in the form of a pronominal particle (particella pronominale). This last case is a topic that we'll cover in our intermediate-level grammar book, which you should consider as a great option to pursue your studies once you complete this workbook.

PRONOMI DIRETTI

Direct pronouns are pronouns that are being used as a direct object (the complement that specifies what or who is the object of the action). Let's look at both the "strong" and "weak" forms, using as an example the verb *amare* (to love), in the second person singular (you love) → "ami". We need to use a verb to make things clearer, so we chose a common one.

EN	IT (forma forte)	IT (forma debole)
You love **me**	Tu ami **me**	Tu **mi** ami
You love **you**	Tu ami **te**	Tu **ti** ami
You love **him/her/it**	Tu ami **lui/lei***	Tu **lo/la** ami
You love **us**	Tu ami **noi**	Tu **ci** ami
You love **you**	Tu ami **voi**	Tu **vi** ami
You love **them**	Tu ami **loro**	Tu **li/le** ami

*Italians normally use *lui/lei* for he/she/it, but, when there's a need to specify that we're not talking about a person, they can recur to the nearly obsolete words *egli/ella* (synonyms of *lui/lei*, but exclusively used for people) and their alternatives for entities that are not sentient: *esso* and *essa*. These two words mean "it", in the two genders.

The two versions, forte and debole, are interchangable and the choice between the two is free. Usually, people choose either one or the other to have a simpler sentence structure, depending on what complements and other words need to be in the sentence, or to highlight a certain part of the sentence.

For example, if we consider "Tu ami me" and "Tu mi ami", the meaning is exactly the same, but in the former sentence the attention is left on "ME", while in the latter the attention is on "LOVES".

PRONOMI INDIRETTI

Pronomi indiretti are used for a type of complement that often calls for a personal pronoun: "complemento di termine". This complement specifies the receiver of the action, as in "Give the pen TO ME"; it is a piece of information that answers the question: "to whom?" or "to what?".

Once again, we'll use a table and a verb to present things in a clearer way. The verb we choose here is "dare" (to give), in the second person singular (you give) → "dai".

EN	IT (forma forte)	IT (forma debole)
You give **me**	Tu dai **a me**	Tu **mi** dai
You give **you**	Tu dai **a te**	Tu **ti** dai
You give **him/her/it**	Tu dai **a lui/lei**	Tu **gli/le** dai
You give **us**	Tu dai **a noi**	Tu **ci** dai
You give **you**	Tu dai **a voi**	Tu **vi** dai
You give **them**	Tu dai **(a) loro**	-*

*Tu gli/le dai (colloquial, formally incorrect)

Pronomi Dimostrativi (Demonstrative Pronouns)

Pronomi dimostrativi are as common as they are simple. They're basically just the same words we saw with aggettivi dimostrativi, but used without the noun.

Examples:

A: "Quale cane?" (*Which dog?*)   B: "Questo cane." (*This dog.*)

A: "Quale cane?" (*Which dog?*)   B: "**Questo**." (*This one.*)

A: "Quale cane?" (*Which dog?*)   B: "Quel cane." (*That dog.*)

A: "Quale cane?" (*Which dog?*)   B: "**Quello**." (*That one.*)

A: "Quale cane?" (*Which dog?*)   B: "Codesto cane." (*This/that dog.*)

A: "Quale cane?" (*Which dog?*)   B: "Codesto." (*This/that one.*)

These pronouns exist in all masculine/feminine and singular/plural forms, so questo/i/a/e and Quel/quello/quella/quei/quegli/quelle (this latter one works like lo/gli or bel/bello).

The Pronoun "Chi"

Some of the adjectives that we discussed in the previous chapters can be used as a pronoun, just like we just saw with *questo* and *quello*. One of them is the adjective "colui", a demonstrative adjective that is quite uncommon and means "he" or "him".

Although uncommon, when it is in the form of a pronoun, it can combine with another common pronoun - *che* = that - to form the pronoun **"chi"**, which means "who" or "whom".

Notice that, although colui is only used for males (with colei being the alternative for female beings), "chi" can be used for either gender.

Let's see some examples:

Who are you? → Chi sei tu? OR Tu chi sei? [*Kee seh-ee too?*]

Who wants pasta? → Chi vuole la pasta? [*Kee voo-oh-leh lah paas-tah?*]

I don't know who you are. → Non so chi sei. [*Nohn soh kee seh-ee*]

Exercises

1. Complete the following lines and add the correct possessive pronoun (like in the example).

[me] Tu ami me .

[you - singular] Tu ami _____.

[her] Tu _____ ami.

[them] Tu ami _____.

[us] Tu _____ ami.

[you - singular] Tu _____ ami.

[him] Tu ami _____.

[you - plural] Tu _____ ami.

[me] Tu _____ ami.

2. Complete the following lines and add the correct possessive pronoun.

[you - singular] Tu _____ ami.

[her] Tu ami _____.

[them] Tu _____ ami.

[us] Tu ami _____.

[you - singular] Tu ami _____.

[him] Tu _____ ami.

[you - plural] Tu ami _____.

[me] Tu ami _____.

3. Complete the following lines and add the correct possessive pronoun (like in the example).

[me] Tu dai qualcosa a me .

[you - singular] Tu dai qualcosa _____.

[her] Tu _____ dai qualcosa.

[them] Tu dai qualcosa _____.

[us] Tu _____ dai qualcosa.

[you - singular] Tu _____ dai qualcosa.

[him] Tu dai qualcosa _____.

[you - plural] Tu _____ dai qualcosa.

[me] Tu _____ dai qualcosa.

4. Complete the following lines and add the correct possessive pronoun.

[you - singular] Tu _____ dai qualcosa.

[her] Tu dai qualcosa _____.

[them] Tu dai _____ qualcosa.

[us] Tu dai qualcosa _____.

[you - singular] Tu dai qualcosa _____.

[him] Tu _____ dai qualcosa.

[you - plural] Tu dai qualcosa _____.

[me] Tu dai qualcosa _____.

5. Complete the translation of the following conversations:

A: Who did you call?   B: I called him.

A: ____ hai chiamato?   B: Ho chiamato _____ .

A: Who is she?   B: She is my best friend.

A: _____?

B: _____.

A: I don't know who talked: B: I think it was them.

A: Non so _____ ha parlato.   B: Penso siano stati _____.

A: No one gave me an answer.   B: Whom did you ask?

A: _____ ha dato una risposta.   B: A _____ hai chiesto?

A: This book belongs to him.   B: Who? That man with the blue shirt? *[blu; camicia]*

A: _____ appartiene a _____ .

B: _____ ? _____ con la _____ ?

6. Rewrite the following sentence using a "pronome diretto" in place of the "pronome indiretto", or vice versa (like in the example).

[Amare = to Love ; Io amo = I love]

Io amo te → <u>Io ti amo</u>

Io li amo → _____

Io amo voi → _____

Io lo amo → _____

Io la amo → _____

Io ci amo → _____

Io le amo → _____

7. Rewrite the following sentence using a "pronome diretto" in place of the "pronome indiretto", or vice versa (like in the example).

[Dire = to Say ; Io dico a te = I say to you]

Io dico a te → <u>Io ti dico</u>

Io dico a loro → _____

Io dico a voi → _____

Io gli dico → _____

Io le dico → _____

Io ti dico → _____

Io ci dico → _____

Answer Keys

1. te, la, loro, ci, ti, lui, vi, mi

2. ti, lei, li, noi, te, lo, voi, me

3. a te, le, a loro, ci, ti, a lui, vi, mi

4. ti, a lei, loro OR a loro, a noi, a te, gli, a voi, a me

5. Chi, lui; Chi è lei?, Lei è la mia migliore amica; Chi, loro; Nessuno mi, chi; Questo libro, lui, Chi, L'uomo, camicia blu.

6. Io amo loro, Io vi amo, Io amo lui, Io amo lei, Io amo noi, Io amo loro (feminine)

7. Io dico loro, Io vi dico, Io dico a lui, Io dico a lei, Io dico a te, Io dico a noi

11. Prepositions and Conjunctions

This chapter will be about very short words: prepositions and conjunctions. Prepositions are a tough nut to crack, not because there's many of them or because they're particularly complicated; it's just that in most cases prepositions are used… randomly, without a clear logic behind the choice.

This means that, in frequent cases, the preposition of choice is not the same, in Italian and English, for a given structure. The only good news is that this is less common with basic expressions and structures, which are our current focus.

With this being said, we'll start with presenting you the basic prepositions (preposizioni semplici - simple prepositions). After that, we'll see how they can join up with articles to form articulated prepositions (preposizioni articolate). Finally, we'll step aside from prepositions for a minute and discuss conjunctions, which is a fairly easy topic.

In the Italian language there are 35 different prepositions, but the situation is actually much simpler than it looks like. Italian prepositions can belong to one of two groups:

- Preposizioni semplici, or simple prepositions, are the basic 9 Italian prepositions, 6 of which can form articulated prepositions.
- Preposizioni articolate are simply prepositions that combine with one of the 6 existing articoli determinativi, which means that there are 32 different possibilities (4 combinations do not exist).

Since articulated prepositions are the result of a combination, you don't need to learn them by heart, as you can simply combine the correct preposition and article.

Preposizioni Semplici

Preposizioni semplici are the basic 9 elements of Italian prepositions. They're all quick and simple, and normally Italians learn them in school in a specific order, which is why most Italians will tell them in the same order if you ask them to name Italian prepositions.

Here they are in a simple table, with the English (most frequent) parallel preposition:

Preposizione Semplice	English Parallel Preposition
Di	Of
A	To
Da	From
In	In
Con	With
Su	On
Per	For
Tra*	Among, between
Fra*	Among, between

* "tra" and "fra" are almost identical and always interchangeable

Try to commit to memory these 9 prepositions, then pass to the next paragraph to see how the first 6 can form preposizioni articolate.

PROPERTY AND POSSESSION

In the meanwhile, let's discuss a short secondary topic: how to talk about property in Italian.

Now that we have seen all the basic prepositions and the pronoun "chi", we have all the basic information to discuss possessions in Italian. The preposition that is used for possessions is "of" → **di**. In Italian there is not an analogue of the English possessive, so this is the only way.

Similarly, when you want to ask "whose" item it is, you simply have to add a preposition "di" before the pronoun "chi" → **di chi?**

Let's look at a couple of examples:

A: Di chi è questo libro?   B: È di Mario.

A: Whose book is this?   B: It's Mario's. (the subject is often implied in Italian)

Ho rubato la penna di Lucia.

I stole Lucia's pen.

Di chi hai paura?

Of whom are you afraid?

Preposizioni Articolate

As the name would suggest, articulated prepositions are prepositions combined with an article, specifically an articolo determinativo. This happens every time the prepositions *di*, *a*, *da*, *in*, and *su* are followed by a noun that needs to be preceded by an article. In these cases, the preposizione articolata is used instead of the preposition and the article.

As you might have noticed, we only mentioned 5 prepositions; that's because the 6th preposition that forms articulated versions, the preposition *con*, only forms it with the articles *il* and *i*, while in the other cases the preposition and article are used as they are, without combining them.

Let's look at all the possible exiting combinations:

Preposizioni articolate						
+	il	lo	la	i	gli	le
di	del	dello	della	dei	degli	delle
a	al	allo	alla	ai	agli	alle
da	dal	dallo	dalla	dai	dagli	dalle
in	nel	nello	nella	nei	negli	nelle
con	col	-	-	coi	-	-
su	sul	sullo	sulla	sui	sugli	sulle

Let's make a few examples to see how they are used:

The book is on the table → Il libro è su+il tavolo → Il libro è sul tavolo [*eel lee-broh èh sool taa-voh-loh*]

The book is in the bag → Il libro è in+la borsa → Il libro è nella borsa [*eel lee-broh èh nehl-lah bor-sah*]

The little girl is with her parents → La bambina è con+i suoi genitori → La bambina è coi suoi genitori [*la baam-bee-nah èh kon ee soo-oh-ee djeh-nee-toh-ree*]

Remember that this does not happen with the prepositions *per*, *tra*, *fra*, and when the preposition *con* is followed by articles other than *il* and *i*:

The bone is for the dog → L'osso è per il cane [*l'ohs-soh èh pehr eel kaa-neh*]

The little girl is with her mom → La bambina è con la sua mamma [*la baam-bee-nah èh kon lah soo-ah maam-mah*]

Conjunctions

Conjunctions are words that help understanding the relation between different parts of a sentence, or different sentences in a longer phrase. There are different types of conjunctions, and the grammar dissertation about conjunctions can be long and very specific.

The good news is that conjunctions work very similarly in Italian and English, and this means that we do not need to get in the deep of grammar analysis to understand how to use them.

Because of this reason, we prefer to avoid presenting a complex analysis of conjunctions to someone who was a beginner before starting this book. Instead, we're going to go through a table with a simple and well-matching translation of the most common examples of a conjunction, without mentioning the different existing types and grouping criteria, as these are the exact same in the two languages anyway.

IT	EN	IT	EN
E	And	Tuttavia	However
Anche	Also, even, too	Sebbene	Although
Inoltre	Moreover	Eccetto	Except
Neanche	Not even	**Quindi**	So
O	Or	Perciò	Because of that
Mentre	While	Infatti	In fact
Oppure	Or differently	Affinché	So that
Altrimenti	Otherwise	**Perché**	Because, why

Se	If	Quando	When
Ma	But	Che	That, who

As you might have noticed, Italians use the same word for "because" and "why" in asking and answering questions:

Q: Why did you kill innocent people?   A: Because I was bored.

Q: Perché hai ucciso persone innocenti?   A: Perché ero annoiato.

Q: *Pehr-kéh aaee ootch-tchee-soh pehr-soh-neh een-noh-tchen-tee?*   A: *Pehr-kéh mee aan-noh-eeaa-voh.*

Q: Why are you throwing feces at monkeys?   A: Because I want revenge!

Q: Perché stai tirando feci alle scimmie?   A: Perché voglio vendetta!

Q: *Pehr-kéh staaee tee-raan-doh pheh-tchee aal-leh sheem-mee-eh?*   A: *Pehr-kéh vo-'yoh vehn-det-tah!*

Finally, let's mention that, whenever the conjunctions *e* and *o*, or the simple preposition *a*, are placed before a word that starts in the same vowel (e, o or a), a letter "d" is added to the conjunction or pronoun:

Lucia e Paola ; Lucia ed Elisa

Lucia o Paola ; Lucia od Orietta

Vado a Dallas ; Vado ad Austin

This can actually be done with any vowel, but nowadays it's common practice to add the D only when it's the exact same vowel as the conjunction/preposition:

Lucia e Anna (preferably) ; Lucia ed Anna (old use, but still rather common)

Exercises

1. Match each Italian preposition with the best-matching English alternative:

    A. Di

    B. A

    C. Da

    D. In

    E. Con

    F. Su

    G. Per

    H. Tra

    I. Fra

    1) With

    2) Between

    3) On

    4) Of

    5) From

    6) To

    7) In

    8) For

2. Write the correct preposizione articolata, when possible, for each given couple of articles and prepositions:

Di + la = _____

Su + lo = _____

Per + il = _____

Con + i = _____

Da + i = _____

Su + gli = _____

A + le = _____

Tra + i = _____

3. Write the correct answer to the question "da dove vieni?" (where are you from?). For each country, the gender and number are specified in brackets:

Dalla Grecia (singular feminine - Grece)

_____ Marocco (singular masculine - Morocco)

_____ Stati Uniti (plural masculine - United States)

_____ Colombia (singular feminine)

_____ Brasile (singular masculine - Brazil)

_____ Australia (singular feminine)

_____ Cina (singular feminine - China)

_____ Giappone (singular masculine - Japan)

_____ Russia (singular feminine)

_____ Seychelles (plural feminine)

4. Write the correct answer to the question "dov'è il libro?" (where's the book?) using the preposition *in* or *su* in the correct articulated version:

_____ sedia (s.f. - chair)

_____ armadio (s.m. - wardrobe)

_____ tavolo (s.m. - table)

_____ zaino (s.m. - backpack)

_____ nostri cuori (p.m. - our hearts)

_____ letto (s.m. - bed)

_____ nostre menti (p.f. - our minds)

_____ tasca (s.f. - pocket)

5. Complete the following sentences using *a* or *da*:

Sono arrivato = I arrived

Partendo = leaving/starting

Sono arrivato _alla_ stazione (s.f. - station) partendo _da_ casa (s.f. home).

Sono arrivato _____ portone (s.m. - big door) partendo _____ cancello (s.m. gate).

Sono arrivato _____ cima (f.s. - top) partendo _____ basi (p.f. basis).

Sono arrivato _____ scogli (p.m. - sea rocks) partendo _____ spiaggia (s.f. beach).

Sono arrivato _____ cassa (s.f. - checkout desk) partendo _____ camerino (s.m. changing room).

6. Write the correct answer to the question "di chi è questa palla?" (whose ball is this?):

_____ cane (s.m. - dog)

_____ maestra (s.f. - female teacher)

_____ muratori (p.m. - laymen)

_____ giocatrici (p.f. - female players)

_____ amici (p.m. - friends)

Answer Keys

1. A4, B6, C5, D7, E1, F3, G8, H2, I2

2. Della, Sullo, Per il, Coi, Dai, Sugli, Alle, Tra i

3. Dal, Dagli, Dalla, Dal, Dall', Dalla, Dal, Dalla, Dalle

4. Sulla, Nell', Sul, Nello, Nei, Sul, Nelle, Nella

5. al, dal; alla, dalle; agli, dalla; alla, dal.

6. Del, Della, Dei, Delle, Degli

12. Adverbs

Italian adverbs are invariable parts of the sentence, meaning that they do not change with gender or number, that specify the meaning of a verb, adjective, or other adverb.

Many adjectives can also be used as adverbs, so let's use the word "molto" (very/a lot), which we've already seen as an adjective, to see some examples of how adverbs are used:

Ho corso molto. → I ran a lot. (modifies a verb)

Il libro è molto grosso. → The book is very big. (modifies an adjective)

Ho corso molto velocemente. →I ran very fast. (modifies an adverb)

As you can see, the word order is variable. So, where do we place it? Well, the rules that determine whether the adverb should be before or after the word they modify can be quite complex and specific. What a beginner should understand is that, in most cases, either of the two possible placings are correct, usually with one of the two just "feeling more natural".

Generally speaking, the preferred placing is BEFORE the adjective, adverb, or noun. If you're unsure, that's what you should go for. The one exception you need to know for now is the case where, like in our first and last examples from above, the sentence ends in the verb which the adverb we introduce modifies. In that case, the adverb goes AFTER the verb.

Types of Adverbs

With this being said, we can move on to presenting the different types of adverbs. We will look at a table with a bunch of common adverbs, which will be grouped for type. You don't need to learn the different types (spoiler: the classification is only partially like in English), so just focus on learning the new words:

Type of adverb	IT	EN	IT	EN
Avverbi di modo (adverbs of manner)	Bene	Well	Lentamente	Slowly
	Male	Not well / badly	Veramente	Truly
	Velocemente	Fast	Realmente	Really
Avverbi di luogo (adverbs of place)	Qui	Here	Dentro	Inside
	Qua	Here	Sopra	Above, Over
	Lì	There	Sotto	Below, Under
	Là	There	Via	Away
	Ci	There	Fuori	Out
Avverbi di tempo (adverbs of time)	Prima	Before	Subito	Immediately
	Poi	After	Sempre	Always
	Ora	Now	Mai	Never
Avverbi di quantità (adverbs of quantity)	Poco	Little, A few	Meno	Less
	Molto	Very, A lot	Solo	Only

	Più	More	Tanto	That much
Avverbi di affermazione (adverbs of confirmation)	Sì	Yes	Certo	Sure
	Certamente	Surely	Davvero	Really
Avverbi di negazione (adverbs of negation)	No	No	Non	Not, Non
Avverbi di dubbio ("adverbs of doubt")	Forse	Maybe	Probabilmente	Probably
Avverbi interrogativi ("interrogative adverbs")	Dove?	Where?	Quando?	When?
	Come?	How?	Perché?	Why?
	Chi?	Who?	Cosa?	What?
Avverbi esclamativi ("exclamatory adverbs")	These are the same words that we've just seen with "interrogative adverbs", but used in an exclamatory connotation.			
Avverbi presentativi ("presentative adverbs")	Ecco	Here … + to be	-	

There are some things in this table at which you should point your attention:
- Avverbi di modo, which are the biggest group, are often formed from the various <u>root words + *mente*</u> as a suffix (e.g slow = lento → lentamente = slowly). The last vowel of the root word gets changed into an A (lento → lenta → lentamente), unless it is an E, in which case the E is kept (veloce → velocemente).
- The <u>adverb "ci"</u> (there) can be mistaken with the pronoun "ci" (we/us/to us). For example: "non ci vengo" = I'm not coming there ; "non ci chiamate" = Don't call us. The verb usually clarifies which of the two words it is. In some cases, unfortunately, it does not: "ci porti" = You take us OR You take (someone or something) there.
- Avverbi di luogo might look redundant, and they are. *Qui* and *qua* are perfect synonyms, and so are *lì* and *là*. Also, the use is 50/50 for both adverbs.
- *Ecco* is the only "presentative" adverb, and it's a fairly common word in Italian. It is used to present something, and in English it corresponds to various forms of "here... + to be", as in: (handing something to someone) "ecco a te" = Here you are ; (presenting to a crowd) "ecco i famosi eroi" = Here are the famous heroes ; (when you see something or someone you were looking/waiting for) "ecco Marco" = Here is Marco. It is also used as a filler word or interjection, basically like "you know" or "I mean" in English.

Bene and Male

Now that we have gone through the basic adjectives and adverbs, it's time to discuss "bene" and "male", which are the words for "good" and "bad". We have already seen some of it, but it's time to directly focus on these 2 little fellows. *Bene* and *male* are not very simple to understand, in the use and in how they make up grammar structures.

Let's start by saying that both words have to be paired with a sort of synonym, which is integral in the use of the word. These synonyms, which should look familiar, are "buono" and "cattivo".

It's worth mentioning that, when it's about the weather, the opposite of bad weather (either *brutto tempo* or *cattivo tempo*) can frequently be nice weather (*bel tempo* - using *bello*). The placing of the adjective before the noun is specific to meteorology. Italians can say *tempo buono*, but it rather means "clement weather" and the adjective goes after the word, because it's a personal opinion and not meteorology. The whole sentence structure usually changes: "C'è bel tempo (Ci è bel tempo - lit. there is good weather)" VS "Il tempo è buono (lit. the weather is ok)".

Now, focusing on *bene/buono* and *male/cattivo*, let's recap and detail the meanings:

Word	Type of word	English equivalent	Examples
Bene *beh-neh*	Adverb (bene or beh, as an interjection)	Well, Fine	*Tutto è bene quel che finisce bene.* All's well that ends well. *Beh, allora addio.* Well, goodbye then. *Sto* bene* I'm fine.
	Noun (il bene, un bene + plurals)	the Right, the Benefit, the Affection, the Love	*La differenza tra il bene e il male.* The difference between right and wrong. *Il bene dell'azienda.*

				The benefit of the company. *Il bene che ti voglio* (to a friend or lover).** The affection I have for you. *Il bene che ti voglio* (to a relative). The love I have for you.
Buono *boo-oh-noh*	Adjective (buono,a,i,e)	Good, Honest, Well-behaving, Good (positive), Good tasting		*Una buona azione.* A good did. *Un uomo buono.* A good/honest man. *Un bambino buono.* A boy who behaves. *Un buon segno.* A good sign (positive). *Una buona cena.* A good-tasting dinner. OR A good dinner (that went well).

				Una buona pizza. A good-tasting pizza. OR A good pizza (in its essence, like good quality or done well).
	Noun (il buono, un buono + feminine and plurals)	the Good, the Good guy		*Il buono, il brutto, il cattivo.* The Good, the Bad and the Ugly. *Non sparare, è uno dei buoni!* Don't shoot, he's one of the good guys (not an enemy)! *Metro Man è il buono in Megamind.* Metro Man is the hero in Megamind. *La damigella in pericolo incontra il buono della storia.* The damsel in distress meets the good guy in the story.
Male *maa-leh*	Adverb (male)	Badly, Wrongly, Impolitely		*Hai fatto male.* You did badly. *Hai messo male la cravatta.* You put on your tie wrongly.

				Mi ha risposto male. He answered me impolitely.
	Noun (il male, un male + plurals)***	the Wrong, the Evil, the Detriment, the Pain		*La differenza tra il bene e il male.* The difference between right and wrong. *Il male nel mondo.* The evil in the world. *Volere il male altrui.* To desire bad things for others. *Ho male alla mano.* I have pain in the hand (my hand hurts).
Cattivo *kaat-tee-voh*	Adjective (cattivo,a,i,e)	Bad, Evil, Mean, Naughty, Bad (negative), Bad tasting		*Una cattiva azione.* A bad did. *Non essere cattivo.* Don't be mean. *Un uomo cattivo.* An evil/bad man.

			Un bambino cattivo. A naughty/disobedient boy. *Un cattivo segno.* A bad sign (negative). *Una cattiva cena.* A bad-tasting dinner. OR A bad dinner (that went poorly). *Una cattiva pizza.* A bad-tasting pizza. OR A bad pizza (in its essence, like low quality or done poorly).
	Noun (il cattivo, un cattivo + feminine and plurals)	the Bad, the Mean, a Bad person, the Felon	*Quello cattivo.* The mean one. *Spara, sono i cattivi!* Shoot, it's the bad guys (enemies)! *Joker è uno dei cattivi di Batman.*

				Joker is one of the felons from Batman.

* Remember that Italians have 2 separate verbs for "to be": "essere" → *Io sono* (I am) ; "stare" → *Io sto* (I am physically).

** This is a consequence of the fact that Italians don't say "I love you" (ti amo - *tee aa-moh*) to relatives and friends; it is only used for romantic love. Instead, they say "Ti voglio bene" (*tee vo-'yo beh-neh*), which expresses affection for someone that's dear to you.

** *mala* does exist but it is a separate noun meaning mob or underworld, it's short for *malavita*.

As you can see, the uses don't always match between Italian and English, that's why we chose to present them as clearly as possible with this table.

One last thing you want to know is that, along with "male", the adverb "malamente" (which comes from *male* + *-mente*) exists, and the two are basically synonyms. The word "benamente" does not exist.

Assessing Your Progress

This is all for now. With this lesson, we have finally seen all of the different types of words that exist in the Italian language, with the only exception of verbs. Our next lessons will be about this final and dense topic, but in future exercises you will still get to practice with all that we have covered so far, as well as with each new topic.

Once you are a little more familiar with verbs, you will have gathered all the required knowledge to understand and formulate most of the basic sentences in Italian. At that point, if you want to start practicing your new skills in a context that is not a grammar book, you can choose to use our handy and informative phrasebook "Italian Phrasebook for Adult Beginners: Speak Italian in 30 Days!", which is perfect to practice with the practical applications of the language, and learn tons of new vocabulary.

Also, the audiobook version of the phrasebook is perfect for practicing pronunciation.

But let's take a minute to take stock of the progress you already made. Right now, you already have built solid language skills, and learned most of the basic words that end up in Italian sentences. The vocabulary you have learned with this book, however, is segmented.

We have gone through nouns, adjectives, pronouns etc., and we learned a similar amount of vocabulary for each category, but in any language there are many more nouns and verbs than there are adjectives or adverbs. Consequently, this means that you currently know a major share of the existing pronouns, articles, and prepositions, for example, but you only know a very little percentage of the existing nouns or adjectives.

This is clearly not your fault, as it is simply a forced consequence of any grammar-driven learning strategy. Regardless of the perspective, the point is that, if we compared you with someone who approached the language differently, you'd generally be more consistent and be more structured with what you know. You'd prevail in structure and consistency, but you'd fall short in practical language skills and uses of the language.

The next chapters will be about verbs. As you start learning verbs, you will be able to handle full sentences in Italian, with endless applications. This will be after the first two lessons, namely after discussing "indicativo presente"- the present tense.

The following lessons will widen your reach in terms of describing events through time, and show you a couple of specific uses for verbs.

As you progress through these chapters, it can be a great choice to start working, in parallel, on other aspects of the language other than grammar. A performing strategy can be pairing grammar studies with a phrasebook, and/or with reading simple stories in Italian. As we believe that's the best strategy, we got you covered with a phrasebook and a simple-story collection, which are both part of this series of books for adult beginners. This is how we believe you should catch up on these parts of the language that our grammar workbook cannot cover.

This combination will grant you great results as you improve in reading, writing, and using the Italian language. The only missing aspects of the language will then be the listening and speaking skills. Let's discuss the doable options for these.

The best way to practice listening and speaking, clearly, is conversing with a native. That can be possible if you visit an Italian-speaking country or if you look for a language-exchange partner, in your city or through one of the many existing apps and communities for language exchange.

A second option, which can be an alternative or an addition to the first one, is turning to immersive content in Italian, such as movies, tv shows or podcasts. For the same principle, the audiobook versions of this book, and of all the other books in this series, can be a great option to practice listening and pronunciation. Our material is specifically designed for beginners, while, when it comes to movies and shows, children's content can be a good option for a beginner, if you can find a show that would keep your interest.

Exercises

1. For each aggettivo qualificativo (descriptive adjective), create the correct adverb by using the suffix -*mente*:

Stupido → <u>Stupidamente</u>   (Stupid→Stupidly)

Dolce → _____ (Sweet→Sweetly)

Intelligente → _____ (Smart→Smartly)

Lento → _____ (Slow→Slowly)

Felice → _____ (Happy→Happily)

Veloce → _____ (Fast→Fast)

Triste → _____ (Sad→Sadly)

Urgente → _____ (Urgent→Urgently)

Calmo → _____ (Calm→Calmly)*

Male → _____ (Bad/Badly→Badly)

Splendido → _____ (Splendid→Splendidly)

*The word required here is very uncommon in actual use.

2. Complete the following sentences using the correct avverbio di luogo:

(Here) Il libro è _____.

(There) Il libro è _____.

(Over) Il libro è _____ al tavolo.

(Under) Il libro è _____ alla sedia.

(Inside) Il libro è _____ all'armadio.

(Above) Questo libro è _____ tutti gli altri.

(Below) Questo libro è _____ le mie aspettative.

3. Add the correct avverbio interrogativo to each question; the answers can point you in the right direction.

A: _____ siamo?   B: Siamo a Roma.

A: _____ sei triste?   B: Perché ho fame.

A: _____ vuoi mangiare?   B: Voglio una Pizza.

A: _____ è lei?   B: È mia sorella.

A: _____ stai?   B: Sto bene.

A: _____ torni?   B: Torno martedì alle 21:00.

A: _____ costa?   B: Costa 5 euro.

4. Complete the following pairs of sentences using *bene* or *buono(a,i,e)*. Remember: *bene* is mostly used as an adverb, so next to verbs, while *buono* is usually an adjective, modifying nouns or expressing qualities. One of the sentences is in English, the other one is in Italian:

A: How's your pizza?   B: Molto _____.

A: How is it going?   B: Sta andando _____.

A: How is your neighbor?   B: È una _____ persona.

A: È _____ fare così?   B: Yes, I think it's the best thing to do.

A: How are you?   B: Sto _____.

A: Non è una _____ idea*.   B: I agree. Terrible idea.

A: È una _____ auto? Funziona** _____?   B: Yes, it drives beautifully.

* It's pronounced *ee-deh-ah*.

**3rd person singular of *funzionare* = to function, to work

5. Complete the following pairs of sentences using *male* or *cattivo(a,i,e)*. Remember: *male* is mostly used as an adverb, so next to verbs, while *cattivo* is usually an adjective, modifying nouns or expressing qualities. One of the sentences is in English, the other one is in Italian:

A: We should invest in crypto!   B: È una _____ idea.

A: Did you hit the car?   B: Sì, ho calcolato _____ le distanze.

A: Chi è il _____ in Superman?   B: It's Lex Luthor.

A: _____ cane!   B: Stop scolding the dog for no reason.

A: Are you in pain?   B: Sì, sto _____.

A: How was your dessert?   B: Aveva un sapore** _____.

A: Is she a bad person?   B: Una _____ persona? Lei è il _____ incarnato!

*= everywhere

**= taste (tip: you can tell the number and gender from the article)

Answer Keys

1. Dolcemente, Intelligentemente, Lentamente, Felicemente, Velocemente, Tristemente, Urgentemente, Calmamente, Malamente, Splendidamente

2. qui OR qua, lì OR là, sopra, sotto, dentro, sopra, sotto

3. Dove, Perché, Cosa, Chi, Come, Quando, Quanto

4. buona; bene; buona; bene; bene; buona; buona, bene

5. cattiva; male; cattivo; Cattivo; male; cattivo; cattiva, male

Verbs: Introduction

Welcome to your first lesson about verbs! The remaining chapters in this book will all be focused lessons that target specific aspects of verb conjugation. It is best to fight verbs one piece at a time, because no single topic is particularly complicated, but together they can be quite a complex enemy to tackle.

The next two lessons will be about Italian verb types and conjugations. These topics are not very practical, and there won't be exercises for these lessons. Nonetheless, we need to cover these topics before getting to actual verbs and use, in order to be able to understand this use.

The first lesson will be about the different types of verbs. In particular, we'll discuss the functional division into the two groups of "verbi transitivi" and "verbi intransitivi", as well as the grouping in -are, -ere, -ire for regular-verbs conjugation.

13. Verb Groups

This lesson will be about verb classification in Italian. It's important to start from here because, on one hand, we want you to be able to see the whole picture and, on the other hand, there are some verbs with specific grammar uses (which are not semantic uses, that concur to the actual meaning) that need to be mentioned.

In particular, we're going to see 3 different types of classification:

- Types of verbs (*tipi di verbi*) → what they do
- Verbal classes (*classi di verbi*) → what can follow
- Conjugation (*coniugazione*) → 3 classes of conjugation for regular verbs

Types of Verbs

Italian verbs can be grouped up based on what they do. We won't get too specific about this classification, but it's important to know that, while most verbs are used to describe an event or to give information about something or someone, there are some verbs that cover a mere grammatical role.

In particular, there are 3 groups of verbs that can operate like this:

- Verbi ausiliari (auxiliary/helper verbs)
- Verbi modali (also known as *verbi servili*, modal OR servile/slave verbs)
- Verbi fraseologici (phraseological/phrasal verbs)

VERBI AUSILIARI

This group of "helper verbs" mainly consists of the verbs *essere*, to be, *and avere*, to have. As we will see, these verbs concur in the construction of composite verbs in the conjugation of all regular and irregular verbs, thus serving the function of helpers.

They do not "add meaning" to the verb; for example, "io ho fatto" (I have done), means that I DID something, and not that I HAVE something (same as in English).

Other than *essere* and *avere*, there are two more verbs that can serve this function: *andare* and *venire* (both irregular verbs). These verbs, which respectively mean "to go" and "to come" can be used in place of *essere* and *avere* in the same constructions. The meaning, however, might change in some cases.

Let's look at some common examples to see what this is all about:

Andare [*va* = it goes]

Va bene! = That's fine/OK! ; È bene! → technically same meaning, but not really used

BUT, also:

Come va? = How is it going?

Va bene! = It's going well

Non mi va = lit. It doesn't go to/with me → = I don't feel like it/I don't want it

Va operato. = It/He needs to be operated (undergo surgery).

Il prato va tagliato = The grass/lawn needs to be cut.

<u>Venire</u> [*vengo* = I come]

Vorrei essere promosso = I'd like/I wish to be promoted.

Vorrei venire promosso = I'd like/I wish to get promoted.

Sono chiamato di continuo = I'm being called continuously

Vengo chiamato di continuo = I'm getting called continuously

In some cases, all three verbs can be used in the same sentence, with basically the same meaning:

Tutto sarà perduto = Everything will be lost OR It will be the end of it all (idiom)

Tutto andrà perduto = Everything will be (consequently) lost

Tutto verrà perduto = Everything will be/get (necessarily) lost

VERBI MODALI

Verbi modali, which used to be called *verbi servili*, are verbs that are put at the service of a second verb, in a way that is partially like what we just saw with verbi ausiliari.

In the Italian language there are 3 different *verbi modali*:

- Potere = to have the possibility to → to be able to / can
- Volere = to want something OR something to happen → to want / to wish
- Dovere = to need to, to have to, must (English can be more specific than Italian here)

The use is actually pretty simple, but unfortunately these are all irregular verbs. Let's look at a few examples, knowing that the first person singular, at the simple present, is, respectively: *posso, voglio, devo*.

Mangio la torta. → I eat the cake.

Posso mangiare la torta. → I can eat the cake.

Voglio mangiare la torta. → I want to eat the cake.

Devo mangiare la torta. → I have to eat the cake.

VERBI FRASEOLOGICI

Phrasal verbs are not as common in Italian as they are in English, but they are used to a certain extent, with higher frequency in the north of the country.

A simple and very common example can be "sto per + infinitive", a specific construction that we're going to discuss and detail in the intermediate-level grammar book of this series.

For now, just know that this phrasal verb can translate into the English "to be going to" future:

I'm going to go / I'm about to go → Sto per andare

I'm going to come / I'm about to come → Sto per venire

I'm going to eat / I'm about to eat → Sto per mangiare

Present continuous is also rendered with a phrasal verb, "sto + gerundive", which we'll discuss in a more specific context (in the intermediate-level grammar book).

Classes of Verbs

Italian verbs are traditionally divided into two classes, depending on their use:

- Verbi transitivi, which hold a direct object
- Verbi intransitivi, which cannot hold a direct object

VERBI TRANSITIVI

Verbi transitivi are all the verbs that can be followed by a direct object, and sometimes they have to, in order to make sense. A simple example can be the verb *aggiustare* (to fix, to repair - it does not usually mean "to adjust"); just like in English, you can't just "fix"; you either "fix SOMETHING" or "fix IT". The same happens in Italian: *aggiustare qualcosa*. It makes sense with a direct object.

When you're unsure, think of the verb, and then try to add "something". To eat something, to kill something, to love something etc., are all verbi transitivi. In most cases, it's the same in Italian and English, as this is more a matter of logic than it is a grammar matter. That's why we considered English examples.

All of these verbs use *avere* as a verbo ausiliare to form composite forms:

[the 1st person singular of *avere* is "ho" at the present tense]

Io ho aggiustato → I fixed / I have fixed

Io ho amato → I loved / I have loved

Io ho ucciso → I killed / I have killed

And the meaning changes if you use *essere* as a verbo ausiliare:

Io sono aggiustato/a → I am fixed

Io sono amato/a → I am loved

Io sono ucciso/a → I am killed

Anticipation: the past particle has to agree in gender and number with the subject when *essere* is the verbo ausiliare. In different words, a girl (or person/being who identifies as female - e.g. Amazon Alexa) would say "sono amata", while a boy would say "sono amato".

VERBI INTRANSITIVI

Verbi intransitivi are all the verbs that <u>cannot be followed by a direct object</u>. Verbs such as to go (andare), to be physically (stare), to arrive (arrivare) etc., cannot be followed by "something" (remember that "I'm feeling sick" → "Sto male" uses *male* as an adverb, hence not a "something"). These verbs can hold other complements, but not a direct object.

All of these verbs use <u>*essere*</u> OR <u>*avere*</u> as a verbo ausiliare to form composite forms:

[the 1st person singular of *essere* is "*sono*" at the present tense]

Io sono andato/a → I went / I have gone

Io sono stato/a → I was / I have been

Io sono arrivato/a → I arrived / I have arrived

The reason why there's a double translation is linked with the use of passato prossimo tense, which we'll see later in this book.

Conjugations Groups

With the only exception of *essere* and *avere*, which follow separate conjugation rules, all regular and irregular Italian verbs belong to one of three conjugation groups:

- Verbs ending in **-are** belong to the 1st conjugation group.
- Verbs ending in **-ere** belong to the 2nd conjugation group.
- Verbs ending in **-ire** belong to the 3rd conjugation group.

Every Italian verb ends in -re in the infinitive, and the letter that precedes this suffix can either be A, E or I. In different words, all verbs either end in -are, -ere, or -ire, and they follow different conjugation rules depending on the case.

For example, let's look at what happens with the second person plural (you guys) for indicativo presente (present simple):

1st group: -are		2nd group: -ere		3rd group: -ire	
Infinitive	Present simple (2nd person plural)	Infinitive	Present simple (2nd person plural)	Infinitive	Present simple (2nd person plural)
Parlare (to speak)	Parl-**a**-te Parlate	Leggere (to read)	Legg-**e**-te Leggete	Sentire (to hear)	Sent-**i**-te Sentite
Portare (to take)	Port-**a**-te Portate	Correre (to run)	Corr-**e**-te Correte	Dormire (to sleep)	Dorm-**i**-te Dormite

Usare (to use)	Us-**a-te** Usate	Prendere (to take)	Pend-**e-te** Prendete	Agire (to act)	Ag-**i-te** Agite
Pagare (to pay)	Pag-**a-te** Pagate	Vedere (to see)	Ved-**e-te** Vedete	Capire (to understand)	Cap-**i-te** Capite

As you can see, the root word is always the infinitive, without the -are, -ere or -ire ending.

This is all for our first introduction. The next chapter will show you the organization and uses of all the various moods and tenses, then we can start learning the actual verbs and conjugations.

In the next lesson, you will also see that there are many different conjugations in Italian, and numerous irregular verbs. This might feel frightening, and daunting, but consider that, albeit Italian conjugations are more complex and detailed than English conjugations, in many cases things are less complicated than it looks.

For example, we chose to use the 2nd person plural in our table because the conjugation is actually identical for the 1st, 2nd and 3rd person singular, and for the 1st person plural, in all three groups.

14. Moods and Tenses

This last introductive chapter will show you the various existing moods and tenses for Italian verbs, and how they are used. You don't need to remember all of them now, as we'll later discuss each tense specifically, at the right time (in this book or in the following intermediate-level grammar book).

Let's start by saying that Italian verbs can be grouped in 2 classes (just for formal reasons), which together are further divided into 7 moods (*modi verbali*); each mood can then have up to 8 tenses (*tempi verbali*) - but only one mood has all 8, with most mood's having just 1 or 2 tenses.

Let's look at this table to have a clearer picture and see how the various moods are used:

Class	Mood	Use
Modi finiti (*moh-dee phee-nee-tee*) "Finite moods"	**Indicativo** 8 tenses	Used to describe an actual event.
	Congiuntivo 4 tenses	Used to describe an opinion or an uncertain event.
	Condizionale 2 tenses	Used to describe an event that is under a certain condition.
	Imperativo 1 tense	Used to give orders.
Modi indefiniti (*moh-dee een-deh-phee-nee-tee*) "Indefinite moods"	**Gerundio** 2 tenses	Used to describe a consideration or to render present continuous
	Participio 2 tenses	It's when the verb is being used as a noun or adjective.
	Infinito 2 tenses	Infinitive, like in English.

Now don't panic. This is the thing in its entirety, so it clearly looks like a lot, but even the highest of mountains gets climbed one step at a time. To reach an A1 grammar level, you're only required to be familiar with 2 tenses of the *Indicativo* mood (*indicativo presente* and *indicativo passato prossimo*), while only 2 more are required for the A2 level (*indicativo imperfetto* and *indicativo futuro*).

This book will cover these 4 tenses, plus a couple more. This will be more than enough to grant you basic language skills with the widest reach possible, without asking you too much.

We'll leave the other tenses for when you're more proficient and ready to handle new information. With this being said, we believe it's better to present you with all of the existing tenses, just so that you know what they look like and when they are used.

This is not ought to help you now, as you should only focus on our 4 target tenses, but seeing the whole picture from the very beginning will help you greatly as you progress and learn more tenses.

So, let's take a look at this table, with the full conjugation of a verb in all the possible moods and tenses. We're going to use the verb "to buy", comprare (*kom-praa-reh*), a regular verb of the first-conjugation group (-are); we're only going to mention the first person singular for each case, for reasons of space, and because our point is just a global presentation:

Mood	Tense	Used to describe an action that...	Example
Indicativo	**Presente**	happens in the present	Compro (*kom-proh*) I buy
	Passato prossimo	just happened and/or still affects the present	Ho comprato (*oh kom-praa-toh*) I have bought
	Imperfetto	was continuous in the past	Compravo (*kom-praa-voh*)

			I was buying OR I used to buy
	Trapassato prossimo	was continuous in a further-back past	Avevo comprato (*aa-veh-voh kom-praa-toh*) I had been buying
	Passato remoto	happened in the past and doesn't significantly affect the present	Comprai (*kom-praa-ee*) I bought
	Trapassato remoto	happened in a further-back past	Ebbi comprato (*ehb-bee kom-praa-toh*) I had bought
	Futuro semplice	will happen	Comprerò (*kom-preh-ròh*) I will buy or I am going to buy
	Futuro anteriore	will have happened	Avrò comprato (*aa-vròh kom-prah-toh*)

			I will have bought
Congiuntivo	**Presente**	is uncertain in the present	(che io) Compri ((*keh eeoh*) *kom-pree*) (should I) buy,
	Passato	was uncertain in the past	(che io) Abbia comprato (*aab-bee-ah kom-praa-toh*) (should I) have bought,
	Imperfetto	was uncertain and continuous in the past	(che io) Comprassi (*kom-praas-see*) Had I bought,
	Trapassato	was uncertain and continuous in a further-back past	(che io) Avessi comprato (*aa-vehs-see kom-praa-toh*)

Mood	Tense	Used to...	Example
			Had I (had) bought
Condizionale	Presente	would happen under a certain condition	Comprerei (*kom-preh-reh-ee*) I would buy
	Passato	would have happened under a certain condition	Avrei comprato (*aa-vreh-ee kom-prah-toh*) I would have bought
Imperativo	Presente	must happen	Compra! (*kom-prah!*) Buy!

Mood	Tense	Used to...	Example
Gerundio	Presente	set a condition	Comprando (*kom-praan-doh*) By buying
	Passato	set a past condition	Avendo comprato

				(*aa-vehn-doh kom-praa-toh*) By having bought
Participio		**Presente**	describe the doer of the action	Comprante (*kom-praan-teh*) He who buys
		Passato	describe the doer of a past action	Avente comprato (*aa-vehn-teh kom-praa-toh*) He who bought
Infinito		**Presente**	describe an action	Comprare (*kom-praa-reh*) To buy
		Passato	describe a past action	Avere comprato (*aa-veh-reh kom-praa-toh*) To have bought

This ends our general presentation. Again, you don't have to learn the various uses now, but it can be useful to have a general understanding of how the thing works.

Our next chapter will target indicativo presente, the most basic of tenses: present simple.

Verbs Conjugation 1

Let's start conjugating verbs! These two lessons will teach you 2 of the *indicativo* tenses: *presente* and *imperfetto*.

From now on, we will take with us a certain group of verbs, which we will conjugate in the tense at matter (for example *indicativo presente* in the next lesson).

These verbs belong to one of three categories:

- Verbs with their own conjugation:
    - Essere (to Be)
    - Avere (to Have)
- Regular verbs:
    - 1st conjugation (-are):
        - Parlare (to Speak OR to Talk)
    - 2nd conjugation (-ere):
        - Leggere (to Read)
    - 3rd conjugation (-ire):
        - Sentire (to Hear)
- Irregular verbs:
    - 1st conjugation (-are):
        - Andare (to Go)
        - Fare (to Do)
        - Stare (to Be physically)
    - 2nd conjugation (-ere):
        - Dovere (to Have to / Must)

- Potere (to Be able to / Can)
- Volere (to Want / to Wish)
- Sapere (to Know how to)
- 3rd conjugation (-ire):
  - Venire (to Come)
  - Dire (to Say)

It's best to study all of them tense by tense, because it's easier than studying a complex table with all the possible conjugations for every single verb.

15. Indicativo Presente

Our first tense will be *indicativo presente*. *Indicativo* is the mood used for events that are actually real, be they present, future, or past events. As you can imagine, it's the most common mood, and it's the one that is used in most situations.

Indicativo presente corresponds to the English present simple (I am, I do). However, since Italians don't have a proper present continuous or "to be going to" future, so sometimes indicativo presente can be used with a future connotation, and it's the context that lets you know. For example:

A: "Hai portato fuori la spazzatura?" B: "Adesso lo faccio!"

B: "Lo faccio domani!"*

A: "Did you take the trash out?" B: "I'll do it now!"

B: "I'm doing it tomorrow!"

*It is also possible to use the future here - "lo farò domani" - but it's less common in this instance because it shows less commitment.

Without further ado, let's move on to the conjugations themselves:

Essere and Avere

Let's see how these verbs are conjugated in the present tense:

Essere

Person	Conjugation	Translation
(1st sin.) **Io**	**Sono** *(Eeoh soh-noh)*	I am
(2nd sin.) **Tu**	**Sei** *(Too seh-ee)*	You are
(3rd sin.) **Lui/Lei**	**È** *(Looee/Leh-ee èh)*	She/He/It is
(1st plur.) **Noi**	**Siamo** *(Noh-ee seeaa-moh)*	We are
(2nd plur.) **Voi**	**Siete** *(Voh-ee see-eh-teh)*	You are
(3rd plur.) **Loro**	**Sono** *(Loh-roh soh-noh)*	They are

Avere

Person	Conjugation	Translation
(1st sin.) **Io**	**Ho** *(Eeoh oh)*	I have
(2nd sin.) **Tu**	**Hai** *(Too aaee)*	You have
(3rd sin.) **Lui/Lei**	**Ha** *(Looee/Leh-ee ah)*	She/He/It has
(1st plur.) **Noi**	**Abbiamo** *(Noh-ee aab-bee-aa-moh)*	We have
(2nd plur.) **Voi**	**Avete** *(Voh-ee aa-veh-teh)*	You have

| (3rd plur.) **Loro** | **Hanno** *(Loh-roh aan-noh)* | They have |

These two verbs have their own conjugation, so they don't really follow any rule and you just have to learn them by heart.

Regular Verbs

Let's now see the rules for regular verbs, using our sample verbs for each group:

1ST CONJUGATION GROUP (-ARE)

Parlare

Person	Conjugation	Translation
(1st sin.) **Io**	**Parl-o** *(Eeoh paar-loh)*	I speak
(2nd sin.) **Tu**	**Parl-i** *(Too paar-lee)*	You speak
(3rd sin.) **Lui/Lei**	**Parl-a** *(Looee/Leh-ee paar-lah)*	She/He/It speaks
(1st plur.) **Noi**	**Parl-iamo** *(Noh-ee paar-leeaa-moh)*	We speak
(2nd plur.) **Voi**	**Parl-a-te** *(Voh-ee paar-laa-teh)*	You speak
(3rd plur.) **Loro**	**Parl-a-no** *(Loh-roh paar-laa-noh)*	They speak

2ND CONJUGATION GROUP (-ERE)

Leggere

Person	Conjugation	Translation
(1st sin.) **Io**	**Legg-o** *(Eeoh leg-goh)*	I read
(2nd sin.) **Tu**	**Legg-i** *(Too ledj-djee)*	You read
(3rd sin.) **Lui/Lei**	**Legg-e** *(Looee/Leh-ee ledj-djeh)*	She/He/It reads
(1st plur.) **Noi**	**Legg-iamo** *(Noh-ee ledj-djeeaa-moh)*	We read
(2nd plur.) **Voi**	**Legg-e-te** *(Voh-ee ledj-djee-teh)*	You read
(3rd plur.) **Loro**	**Legg-o-no** *(Loh-roh leg-goh-noh)*	They read

We underlined the parts that differ from the first-conjugation rules.

3RD CONJUGATION GROUP (-IRE)

Sentire

Person	Conjugation	Translation
(1st sin.) **Io**	**Sent-o** *(Eeoh sehn-toh)*	I hear
(2nd sin.) **Tu**	**Sent-i** *(Too sehn-tee)*	You hear
(3rd sin.) **Lui/Lei**	**Sent-e** *(Looee/Leh-ee sehn-teh)*	She/He/It hears

(1st plur.) **Noi**	**Sent-iamo** *(Noh-ee sehn-teeaa-moh)*	We hear
(2nd plur.) **Voi**	**Sent-i-te** *(Voh-ee sehn-tee-teh)*	You hear
(3rd plur.) **Loro**	**Sent-o-no** *(Loh-roh sehn-toh-noh)*	They hear

We underlined the parts that differ from the first-conjugation rules.

Irregular Verbs

Finally, our chosen group of irregular verbs:

Andare

Person	Conjugation	Translation
(1st sin.) **Io**	**Vad-o** *(Eeoh vaa-doh)*	I go
(2nd sin.) **Tu**	**Va-i** *(Too vaa-ee)*	You go
(3rd sin.) **Lui/Lei**	**V-a** *(Looee/Leh-ee vah)*	She/He/It goes
(1st plur.) **Noi**	**And-iamo** *(Noh-ee aan-deeaa-moh)*	We go
(2nd plur.) **Voi**	**And-a-te** *(Voh-ee aan-daa-teh)*	You go
(3rd plur.) **Loro**	**Van-no** *(Loh-roh vaan-noh)*	They go

We underlined the parts that differ from the conjugation of regular verbs from this group.

Fare

Person	Conjugation	Translation
(1st sin.) **Io**	**Facci-o** *(Eeoh phaatch-tchoh)*	I do
(2nd sin.) **Tu**	**Fa-i** *(Too phaa-ee)*	You do
(3rd sin.) **Lui/Lei**	**F-a** *(Looee/Leh-ee phah)*	She/He/It does
(1st plur.) **Noi**	**Facc-iamo** *(Noh-ee phaatch-tcheeaa-moh)*	We do
(2nd plur.) **Voi**	**Fa-te** *(Voh-ee phaa-teh)*	You do
(3rd plur.) **Loro**	**Fan-no** *(Loh-roh phaan-noh)*	They do

We underlined the parts that differ from the conjugation of regular verbs from this group.

Stare

Person	Conjugation	Translation
(1st sin.) **Io**	**St-o** *(Eeoh stoh)*	I am physically
(2nd sin.) **Tu**	**Sta-i** *(Too staa-ee)*	You are physically
(3rd sin.) **Lui/Lei**	**St-a** *(Looee/Leh-ee stah)*	She/He/It is physically

(1st plur.) **Noi**	**St-iamo** *(Noh-ee steeaa-moh)*	We are physically
(2nd plur.) **Voi**	**St-a-te** *(Voh-ee staa-teh)*	You are physically
(3rd plur.) **Loro**	**St-an-no** *(Loh-roh staan-noh)*	They are physically

We underlined the parts that differ from the conjugation of regular verbs from this group.

Dovere

Person	Conjugation	Translation
(1st sin.) **Io**	**Dev-o** *(Eeoh deh-voh)*	I must
(2nd sin.) **Tu**	**Dev-i** *(Too deh-vee)*	You must
(3rd sin.) **Lui/Lei**	**Dev-e** *(Looee/Leh-ee deh-veh)*	She/He/It must
(1st plur.) **Noi**	**Dobb-iamo** *(Noh-ee Dohb-beeaa-moh)*	We must
(2nd plur.) **Voi**	**Dov-e-te** *(Voh-ee doh-vee-teh)*	You must
(3rd plur.) **Loro**	**Dev-o-no** *(Loh-roh deh-voh-noh)* OR Debb-o-no (less common)	They must

We underlined the parts that differ from the conjugation of regular verbs from this group.

Potere

Person	Conjugation	Translation
(1st sin.) Io	**Poss**-o (Eeoh pohs-soh)	I can
(2nd sin.) Tu	**Puo**-i (Too poo-oh-ee)	You can
(3rd sin.) Lui/Lei	**Può** (Looee/Leh-ee poo-òh)	She/He/It can
(1st plur.) Noi	**Poss**-iamo (Noh-ee pohs-seeaa-moh)	We can
(2nd plur.) Voi	Pot-e-te (Voh-ee poh-teh-teh)	You can
(3rd plur.) Loro	**Poss**-o-no (Loh-roh pohs-soh-noh)	They can

We underlined the parts that differ from the conjugation of regular verbs from this group.

Volere

Person	Conjugation	Translation
(1st sin.) Io	**Vogli**-o (Eeoh voh-'yeeoh)	I want
(2nd sin.) Tu	**Vuo**-i (Too voo-oh-ee)	You want
(3rd sin.) Lui/Lei	**Vuol**-e (Looee/Leh-ee voo-oh-leh)	She/He/It wants

Person	Conjugation	Translation
(1st plur.) **Noi**	**Vogl**-iamo *(Noh-ee voh-'yeeaa-moh)*	We want
(2nd plur.) **Voi**	**Vol**-e-te *(Voh-ee voh-leh-teh)*	You want
(3rd plur.) **Loro**	**Vogli**-o-no *(Loh-roh voh-'yeeoh-noh)*	They want

We underlined the parts that differ from the conjugation of regular verbs from this group.

<u>Sapere</u>

Person	Conjugation	Translation
(1st sin.) **Io**	**S**-o *(Eeoh soh)*	I know
(2nd sin.) **Tu**	**Sa**-i *(Too saaee)*	You know
(3rd sin.) **Lui/Lei**	**Sa** *(Looee/Leh-ee sah)*	She/He/It knows
(1st plur.) **Noi**	**Sapp**-iamo *(Noh-ee saap-peeaa-moh)*	We know
(2nd plur.) **Voi**	**Sap**-e-te *(Voh-ee saa-peh-teh)*	You know
(3rd plur.) **Loro**	**San**-no *(Loh-roh saan-noh)*	They know

We underlined the parts that differ from the conjugation of regular verbs from this group.

Venire

Person	Conjugation	Translation
(1st sin.) **Io**	**Veng-o** *(Eeoh vehn-goh)*	I come
(2nd sin.) **Tu**	**Vien-i** *(Too vee-eh-nee)*	You come
(3rd sin.) **Lui/Lei**	**Vien-e** *(Looee/Leh-ee vee-eh-neh)*	She/He/It comes
(1st plur.) **Noi**	**Ven-iamo** *(Noh-ee vehn-eeaa-moh)*	We come
(2nd plur.) **Voi**	**Ven-i-te** *(Voh-ee vehn-ee-teh)*	You come
(3rd plur.) **Loro**	**Ven-go-no** *(Loh-roh vehn-goh-noh)*	They come

We underlined the parts that differ from the conjugation of regular verbs from this group.

Dire

Person	Conjugation	Translation
(1st sin.) **Io**	**Dic-o** *(Eeoh dee-koh)*	I say
(2nd sin.) **Tu**	**Dic-i** *(Too dee-tchee)*	You say
(3rd sin.) **Lui/Lei**	**Dic-e** *(Looee/Leh-ee dee-tcheh)*	She/He/It says

(1st plur.) **Noi**	**Dic**-iamo *(Noh-ee dee-tcheeaa-moh)*	We say
(2nd plur.) **Voi**	**D**-**i**-te *(Voh-ee dee-teh)*	You say
(3rd plur.) **Loro**	**Dic**-o-no *(Loh-roh dee-koh-noh)*	They say

We underlined the parts that differ from the conjugation of regular verbs from this group.

This is all for *indicativo presente*! Our advice is to focus on *essere*, *avere*, and the 3 regular conjugations. As for the irregular verbs, these are all basic verbs, so it's worth learning them, but you can wait if it feels too much now.

With irregular verbs, focus your attention on the root word(s), since that's usually where things stop following the rules.

Exercises

1. Complete the following sentences with the correct form of either *essere* or *avere*, in the present tense (indicativo presente).

Io _____ Mario.

Luca _____ un cane.

Luca e Paolo _____ amici miei.

Loro _____ una bella casa.

Tu _____ un libro?

Voi _____ amici di Paolo?

2. Complete the following sentences with the correct form of either *essere* or *avere*, in the present tense (indicativo presente).

Noi _____ due gatti.

Tu _____ americano?

Io e Paolo _____ amici.

Lucia _____ una bella ragazza.

Io _____ un problema.

Tu e Luca _____ amici in comune?

3. Conjugate the following REGULAR verbs in the present tense (indicativo presente):

Verb	Meaning	Required person	Answer
Amare	to Love	1st person singular	
Pensare	to Think	3rd person plural	
Viaggiare	to Travel	2nd person plural	
Aprire	to Open	2nd person singular	
Usare	to Use	1st person singular	
Servire	to Serve	2nd person singular	
Cercare	to Look for	3rd person singular	
Piangere	to Cry	1st person plural	

Trovare	to Find	1st person singular	
Decidere	to Decide	2nd person singular	
Visitare	to Visit	3rd person singular	
Ridere	to Laugh	1st person singular	
Imparare	to Learn	2nd person plural	
Promettere	to Promise	3rd person singular	
Rompere	to Break	3rd person plural	
Mettere	to Put	1st person plural	
Seguire	to Follow	3rd person singular	

4. Complete the following sentences with the correct form of the verb in brackets, in the present tense (indicativo presente).

(venire) Noi _____ dall'Italia.

(fare) Tu mi _____ ridere.

(stare) Io e Paolo _____ bene.

(sapere) Lucia _____ cucinare bene. (= to cook)

(potere) Io _____ andare.

(volere) Tue e Luca _____ il gelato?

5. Complete the following sentences with the correct form of the verb in brackets, in the present tense (indicativo presente).

(andare) Noi _____ a Parigi.

(fare) Loro _____ degli ottimi caffè.

(andare) Io e Paolo _____ a Roma.

(dovere) Lucia _____ mangiare di più.

(dire) Io _____ questo.

(venire) Tu e Luca _____ alla festa? (= to the party)

Answer keys

1. sono, ha (OR è), sono, hanno, hai, siete

2. abbiamo (OR siamo), sei, siamo (OR abbiamo), è (OR ha), ho OR sono, avete

3.

Verb	Meaning	Required person	Answer
Amare	to Love	1st person singular	Io **amo**
Pensare	to Think	3rd person plural	Loro **pensano**
Viaggiare	to Travel	2nd person plural	Voi **viaggiate**
Aprire	to Open	2nd person singular	Tu **apri**
Usare	to Use	1st person singular	Io **uso**
Servire	to Serve	2nd person singular	Tu **servi**
Cercare	to Look for	3rd person singular	Lui/Lei **cerca**
Piangere	to Cry	1st person plural	Noi **piangiamo**
Trovare	to Find	1st person singular	Io **trovo**

Decidere	to Decide	2nd person singular	Tu **decidi**
Visitare	to Visit	3rd person singular	Lui/Lei **visita**
Ridere	to Laugh	1st person singular	Io **rido**
Imparare	to Learn	2nd person plural	Voi **imparate**
Promettere	to Promise	3rd person singular	Lui/Lei **promette**
Rompere	to Break	3rd person plural	Loro **rompono**
Mettere	to Put	1st person plural	Noi **mettiamo**
Seguire	to Follow	3rd person singular	Lui/Lei **segue**

4. veniamo, fai, stiamo, sa, posso, volete

5. andiamo, fanno, andiamo, deve, dico, venite

16. Indicativo Passato Prossimo

Passato prossimo is a past tense with a geographic difference in use. It is used a lot more frequently in the north of the country than it is in the south, because in the north people use it for both past simple and present perfect. Although the southern use is to be considered more correct, the grammar behind the choice is debatable.

Technically, *passato prossimo* is a tense that is <u>used for past actions that still have an influence on the present</u>, and it can be compared to the English present perfect. The presence or absence of that influence is the debatable part.

In northern Italy, people tend to consider almost any past action as still influencing the present, so they use *passato prossimo* for both present perfect and past simple all the time. In the south, however, most people use *passato remoto* for past simple, as a correct grammar would suggest.

As a learner, what should matter to you from all this story is that, in practical terms, this tense can be used for both present perfect and past simple in almost any occasion, except for very formal and specific circumstances, that will most likely never interest you. Also, even when used correctly. passato prossimo can be correct in cases where in English we'd use present simple. In the following conjugation tables, we'll mention the double translation (only for the 1st person singular).

Composite Verbs

Passato prossimo is a COMPOSITE VERB that can either have *essere* or *avere* as an auxiliary verb; this mostly depends on whether the verb is *transitivo* or *intransitivo*, as we mentioned in a previous lesson.

Generally speaking, if the verb is followed by a direct object (even when it is implied), it's being used as *transitivo* and the auxiliary verb will be *avere*, at indicativo presente in this case (*ho, hai, ha, abbiamo, avete, hanno*).

Remember that direct object (*complemento oggetto*) is typically the only complement that is not preceded by a preposition, so it's pretty easy to spot one.

If the verb cannot be followed by a direct object, it's being used as *intransitivo* and the auxiliary verb can be either *avere* or *essere* (*sono, sei, è, siamo, siete, sono*).

So, when is *essere* used as a helper verb? There are a few different cases, and in all these cases the verb is *intransitivo,* or used as such. In particular, *essere* is used when:

- We have a verb of movement, such as to go, to leave, to arrive etc. (*andare, partire, arrivare...*). However, there are exceptions, like *camminare* and *viaggiare* (to walk and to travel).

- We have a <u>verb of state, or change of state</u>, such as to be, sto stay, to change, to become etc. (*essere, stare, cambiare, diventare…*)
- The subject is a <u>passive receiver of the action</u>, such as to be born, to grow up, (*nascere, crescere*).
- The verb is a *<u>verbo riflessivo</u>*; these are a specific type of verbs that always have the subject as a direct object too, for example lavarsi (to wash oneself) or prepararsi (to get oneself ready). As you can see, these are composite forms (lavare + si = lavarsi).
- The <u>verb is used passively</u>: Io ho ucciso (I have killed), Io sono ucciso (I am killed). Notice that the first verb is in the *passato prossimo* tense, but the second one is actually a passive form in the *presente* tense (I have killed yesterday, I am killed now).
- The verb is a *<u>verbo modale</u>*, only when supporting a verb that needs *essere* as an auxiliary verb (on their own, they all need *avere*).

Other than the auxiliary verb, this tense is made with the use of *participio passato*, past participle, a different tense that we'll discuss in greater detail later in this book. For now, just know that the recurring part of *passato prossimo* is the *participio passato* of that verb. Also, consider that this tense gets to vary in gender and number, with the usual endings -*o,a,i,e* (but *verbi transitivi* often don't change).

Essere and Avere

Let's now move our attention to the conjugation tables:

<u>Essere</u> [Participio passato: stato,a,i,e]

Person	Conjugation	Translation
(1st sin.) **Io**	**Sono stato** *(Eeoh soh-noh staa-toh)*	I have been / I was
(2nd sin.) **Tu**	**Sei stato** *(Too seh-ee staa-toh)*	You have been

(3rd sin.) **Lui/Lei**	**È stato** (*Looee/Leh-ee èh staa-toh*)	She/He/It has been
(1st plur.) **Noi**	**Siamo stati** (*Noh-ee seeaa-moh staa-tee*)	We have been
(2nd plur.) **Voi**	**Siete stati** (*Voh-ee see-eh-teh staa-tee*)	You have been
(3rd plur.) **Loro**	**Sono stati** (*Loh-roh soh-noh staa-tee*)	They have been

Avere [Participio passato: avuto,a,i,e]

Person	Conjugation	Translation
(1st sin.) **Io**	**Ho avuto** (*Eeoh oh aa-voo-toh*)	I have had / I had
(2nd sin.) **Tu**	**Hai avuto** (*Too aaee aa-voo-toh*)	You have had
(3rd sin.) **Lui/Lei**	**Ha avuto** (*Looee/Leh-ee ah aa-voo-toh*)	She/He/It has had
(1st plur.) **Noi**	**Abbiamo avuto** (*Noh-ee aab-bee-aa-moh aa-voo-toh*)	We have had
(2nd plur.) **Voi**	**Avete avuto** (*Voh-ee aa-veh-teh aa-voo-toh*)	You have had
(3rd plur.) **Loro**	**Hanno avuto** (*Loh-roh aan-noh aa-voo-toh*)	They have had

These two verbs have their own conjugation, so they don't really follow any rule and you just have to learn them by heart.

Regular Verbs

Let's now see the rules for regular verbs, using our sample verbs for each group:

1ST CONJUGATION GROUP (-ARE)

<u>Parlare</u> [Participio passato: parlato,a,i,e]

Person	Conjugation	Translation
(1st sin.) **Io**	**Ho parlato** *(Eeoh oh paar-lah-toh)*	I have talked / I talked
(2nd sin.) **Tu**	**Hai parlato** *(Too aaee paar-lah-toh)*	You have talked
(3rd sin.) **Lui/Lei**	**Ha parlato** *(Looee/Leh-ee ah paar-lah-toh)*	She/He/It has talked
(1st plur.) **Noi**	**Abbiamo parlato** *(Noh-ee aab-bee-aa-moh paar-lah-toh)*	We have talked
(2nd plur.) **Voi**	**Avete parlato** *(Voh-ee aa-veh-teh paar-lah-toh)*	You have talked
(3rd plur.) **Loro**	**Hanno parlato** *(Loh-roh aan-noh paar-lah-toh)*	They have talked

2ND CONJUGATION GROUP (-ERE)

<u>Leggere</u> [Participio passato: letto,a,i,e]

Person	Conjugation	Translation
(1st sin.) **Io**	**Ho letto** *(Eeoh oh leht-toh)*	I have read / I read
(2nd sin.) **Tu**	**Hai letto** *(Too aaee leht-toh)*	You have read
(3rd sin.) **Lui/Lei**	**Ha letto** *(Looee/Leh-ee ah leht-toh)*	She/He/It has read
(1st plur.) **Noi**	**Abbiamo letto** *(Noh-ee aab-bee-aa-moh leht-toh)*	We have read
(2nd plur.) **Voi**	**Avete letto** *(Voh-ee aa-veh-teh leht-toh)*	You have read
(3rd plur.) **Loro**	**Hanno letto** *(Loh-roh aan-noh leht-toh)*	They have read

There are no differences with the first-conjugation rules.

3RD CONJUGATION GROUP (-IRE)

<u>Sentire</u> [Participio passato: sentito,a,i,e]

Person	Conjugation	Translation
(1st sin.) **Io**	**Ho sentito** *(Eeoh oh sehn-tee-toh)*	I have heard / I heard

(2nd sin.) **Tu**	**Hai sentito** *(Too aaee sehn-tee-toh)*	You have heard
(3rd sin.) **Lui/Lei**	**Ha sentito** *(Looee/Leh-ee ah sehn-tee-toh)*	She/He/It has heard
(1st plur.) **Noi**	**Abbiamo sentito** *(Noh-ee aab-bee-aa-moh sehn-tee-toh)*	We have heard
(2nd plur.) **Voi**	**Avete sentito** *(Voh-ee aa-veh-teh sehn-tee-toh)*	You have heard
(3rd plur.) **Loro**	**Hanno sentito** *(Loh-roh aan-noh sehn-tee-toh)*	They have heard

There are no differences with the first-conjugation rules.

Irregular Verbs

Finally, our chosen group of irregular verbs. Mind that irregular verbs, when used in composite tenses, act just like regular verbs, so we are going to show you the whole conjugation for "andare" and "stare", but with the other ones we'll just mention the auxiliary verb and the *participio passato*, even though it might even be regular (not that you're able to tell yet - we're going to study *participio passato* in the final chapters of this book).

Andare [Participio passato: andato,a,i,e] → verb of movement → aux: *essere*

Person	Conjugation	Translation
(1st sin.) **Io**	**Sono andato** *(Eeoh soh-noh aan-daa-toh)*	I have gone

(2nd sin.) **Tu**	**Sei andato** *(Too seh-ee aan-daa-toh)*	You have gone
(3rd sin.) **Lui/Lei**	**È andato** *(Looee/Leh-ee èh aan-daa-toh)*	She/He/It has gone
(1st plur.) **Noi**	**Siamo andati** *(Noh-ee seeaa-moh aan-daa-tee)*	We have gone
(2nd plur.) **Voi**	**Siete andati** *(Voh-ee see-eh-teh aan-daa-tee)*	You have gone
(3rd plur.) **Loro**	**Sono andati** *(Loh-roh soh-noh aan-daa-tee)*	They have gone

Stare [Participio passato: stato,a,i,e] → verb of state → aux: *essere*

Person	Conjugation	Translation
(1st sin.) **Io**	**Sono stato** *(Eeoh soh-noh staa-toh)*	I have been / I was (physically)
(2nd sin.) **Tu**	**Sei stato** *(Too seh-ee staa-toh)*	You have been (physically)
(3rd sin.) **Lui/Lei**	**È stato** *(Looee/Leh-ee èh staa-toh)*	She/He/It has been (physically)
(1st plur.) **Noi**	**Siamo stati** *(Noh-ee seeaa-moh staa-tee)*	We have been (physically)
(2nd plur.) **Voi**	**Siete stati** *(Voh-ee see-eh-teh staa-tee)*	You have been (physically)

(3rd plur.) **Loro**	**Sono stati** (Loh-roh soh-noh staa-tee)	They have been (physically)

Notice that this conjugation is the same as *verbo essere*. The two verbs basically merge in all composite tenses, showing no difference in meaning whatsoever. Let's see an example:

"Io sono buono" = "I'm a good person", "I'm easy to deal with", "I taste good".

"Io sto buono" = "I behave well", "I stay quiet" → (I'm physically a good person)

"Io sono stato buono" = "I was a good person", "I stayed quiet"...(all of the meanings)

Fare [Participio passato: fatto,a,i,e] → aux: *avere*

Dovere [Participio passato: dovuto,a,i,e] → aux: *avere* (except when used as a modal verb with verbs that require *essere*)

e.g. Ho dovuto ; Ho dovuto leggere ; Sono dovuto andare

Potere [Participio passato: potuto,a,i,e] → aux: *avere* (except when used as a modal verb with verbs that require *essere*)

e.g. Ho potuto ; Ho potuto leggere ; Sono potuto andare

Volere [Participio passato: voluto,a,i,e] → aux: *avere* (except when used as a modal verb with verbs that require *essere*)

e.g. Ho voluto ; Ho voluto leggere ; Sono voluto andare

Sapere [Participio passato: saputo,a,i,e] → aux: *avere*

Venire [Participio passato: venuto,a,i,e] → verb of movement → aux: *essere*

Dire [Participio passato: detto,a,i,e] → aux: *avere*

As you might have noticed from the tables, sometimes the participio passato changes in number (and it also has to change in gender), while sometimes it does not. This is a rather complex topic, but for now let's simplify things and say that, generally speaking:

- verbs that use *essere* as an auxiliary verb, when they are used in a composite form, have to agree in gender (and number obviously) with the subject.

If I/we are girls:

Io sono stat<u>a</u> male. ;   Noi siamo stat<u>e</u> male.

- *verbi transitivi* that use *avere* as an auxiliary verb, when used in a composite form, might need to agree in gender and number with the direct object, especially when the direct object is placed before the verb. Let's say that the interlocutor "you" is a girl, or are girls:

Ho sentito te. ;   Ti ho sentit<u>a</u>.

Ho amato te. ;   Ti ho amat<u>a</u>.

Ho ucciso voi ;   Vi ho uccis<u>e</u>.

This topic is a little too advanced for your current level, but we thought it was best to point it out so that you can start noticing examples of this, and start gathering practical information on its use (that will come handy when you study this in the future).

Exercises

1. Complete the following sentences with the correct form of either *essere* or *avere*, in the *passato prossimo* tense. Notice that in some cases we'd use past simple in English.

Io _____ un soldato. (*sol-daa-toh*= a soldier)

Luca _____ un cane.

Luca e Paolo _____ un incidente. (*een-tchee-den-teh* = an accident)

Loro _____ a Roma.

Tu _____ dei figli? (*phee-'yee*= sons)

Voi _____ dei problemi?

2. Complete the following sentences with the correct form of either *essere* or *avere*, in the *passato prossimo* tense.

Noi _____ due gatti.

Tu _____ in India?

Io e Paolo _____ a scuola. (*skoo-oh-lah* = school)

Lucia _____ a New York.

Io _____ un problema.

Tu e Luca _____ in giardino? (*djaar-dee-noh* = garden)

3. Complete the following sentences with the correct form of the verb in brackets, in the *passato prossimo* tense.

(arrivare) Noi _____ dall'Italia.

(fare) Tu mi _____ ridere.

(stare) Io e Paolo _____ bene.*

(leggere) Lucia _____ un libro.

(potere) Io non _____ andare. (tip: what kind of verb is this modal verb helping?)

(volere) Tue e Luca _____ un bambino? (tip: is *volere* being used as a modal?)

*This is also used as an idiomatic expression. The literal meaning is "we have been well", and it is used to say "it was nice", usually in the context of "we enjoyed the stay/time spent there" or "we enjoyed the time spent with someone/each other".

4. Complete the following sentences with the correct form of the verb in brackets, in the *passato prossimo* tense.

(andare) Noi _____ a Parigi.

(amare) Loro _____ i miei muffin.

(parlare) Io e Paolo _____.

(sentire) Lucia _____ un brutto suono. (*soo-oh-noh* = sound)
(dire) Io _____ questo?
(venire) Tu e Luca _____ alla festa? (= to the party)

5. Translate the following sentences into English:

Sono stato bravo.
_____

Ho parlato con Marco.
_____

Marta, un amica di Maria, ha avuto un incidente.
_____

Chi ha parlato?
_____

Ti ho amata, ma il passato è il passato.
_____

Come dici: "sono venuto" in inglese?
_____

6. Translate the following sentences into Italian (use *passato prossimo* for all English past tenses):

Who has been to Milan?
_____

I've had an accident.
_____

I said that, but I could not do that.
_____

Who talked?
_____

When have you been there?
_____

Why did you go?

Answer Keys

1. sono stato, ha avuto, hanno avuto, sono stati/e, hai avuto, avete avuto

2. abbiamo avuto, sei stato/a, siamo stati, è stata, ho avuto (OR sono stato/a), siete stati

3. siamo arrivati, hai fatto/a ridere, siamo stati, ha letto, sono potuto/a, avete voluto

4. siamo andati/e, hanno amato, abbiamo parlato, ha sentito, ho detto, siete venuti

5. I was/have been good OR I behaved well. I (have) talked to/with Marco. Marta, a friend of Maria's, (has) had an accident. Who (has) talked? I (have) loved you, but the past is the past. How do you say: "I came/have come" in English?

6. Chi è stato/a a Milano? Ho avuto un incidente. Ho detto quello, ma non ho potuto fare quello (OR L'ho detto, ma non ho potuto fare quello. Chi ha parlato? Quando sei stato/a/i/e lì/là (OR quando ci sei stato/a/i/e)? Perché sei andato(a) / siete andati(e).

Verbs Conjugation 2

In the previous chapters, we learned how to articulate sentences in order to describe events that happen in the present, or that have happened in the past. These following two lessons will teach you how to describe events that will happen in the future, and how to be more specific about past events.

In particular, we will study *indicativo imperfetto*, a past tense that is used to describe actions that were continuous in the past. This tense does not really translate with past continuous, or with any other English tense, as it is usually used to say "I used to…".

Indicativo futuro is easier under this viewpoint, as it perfectly matches the English future simple (with very few exceptions). However, both tenses have their specific conjugations, which we need to learn.

17. Indicativo Imperfetto

Imperfetto is a past tense, but it is not used to describe events that HAPPENED in the past, but rather for events that TOOK PLACE in the past. These are events that were not isolated in time, that did not happen in a moment, but that lasted for a prolonged amount of time.

Depending on the case, this tense can be translated with the English past continuous:

Sono caduto mentre correvo. → I fell while I was running. (cadere = to fall)

Mi ha chiamato mentre mangiavo. → He/She called while I was eating. (chiamare = to call)

In some cases, however, it translates into the English "used to".

Quando ero piccolo, giocavo a calcio → When I was little, I used to play soccer

Prendevo il bus per andare al lavoro → I used to take the bus to go to work

One last thing to mention is that, sometimes, in English we use past simple for sentences in which Italians would use *imperfetto*, as they would consider the action to be protracted in time. For example:

I was the best in math → Ero il migliore in matematica. (this is not a single event)

I was on the phone → Ero al telefono. (phone calls last some time)

As we mentioned some time ago, *imperfetto* is also used, in popular (incorrect) use, for all the constructions that would require the use of *congiuntivo* and *condizionale*:

Se fossi in* te, non lo farei. = If I were you, I wouldn't do it.

Se ero te, non lo facevo. = If I was you, I ain't do it.

*idiomatic use of a preposition "If I were IN you, in your shoes"

Let's see how verbs are conjugated in this tense!

Essere and Avere

Essere

Person	Conjugation	Translation
(1st sin.) **Io**	**Er-o** *(Eeoh eh-roh)*	I was / used to be / was +ing
(2nd sin.) **Tu**	**Er-i** *(Too eh-ree)*	You were
(3rd sin.) **Lui/Lei**	**Er-a** *(Looee/Leh-ee eh-rah)*	She/He/It was

(1st plur.) **Noi**	**Er-a-vamo** *(Noh-ee eh-raa-vaa-moh)*	We were
(2nd plur.) **Voi**	**Er-a-vate** *(Voh-ee eh-raa-vaa-teh)*	You were
(3rd plur.) **Loro**	**Er-a-no** *(Loh-roh eh-raa-noh)*	They were

Avere

Person	Conjugation	Translation
(1st sin.) **Io**	**Av-e-vo** *(Eeoh aa-veh-voh)*	I had / used to have
(2nd sin.) **Tu**	**Av-e-vi** *(Too aa-veh-vee)*	You had
(3rd sin.) **Lui/Lei**	**Av-e-va** *(Looee/Leh-ee aa-veh-vah)*	She/He/It had
(1st plur.) **Noi**	**Av-e-vamo** *(Noh-ee aa-veh-vaa-moh)*	We had
(2nd plur.) **Voi**	**Av-e-vate** *(Voh-ee aa-veh-vaa-teh)*	You had
(3rd plur.) **Loro**	**Av-e-vano** *(Loh-roh aa-veh-vaa-noh)*	They had

Avere is conjugated like a regular verb of the 2nd conjugation group, in this tense.

Regular Verbs

Let's now see the rules for regular verbs, using our sample verbs for each group:

1ST CONJUGATION GROUP (-ARE)

Parlare

Person	Conjugation	Translation
(1st sin.) **Io**	**Parl-a-vo** *(Eeoh paar-laa-voh)*	I was speaking / used to speak
(2nd sin.) **Tu**	**Parl-a-vi** *(Too paar-laa-vee)*	You were speaking
(3rd sin.) **Lui/Lei**	**Parl-a-va** *(Looee/Leh-ee paar-laa-vah)*	She/He/It was speaking
(1st plur.) **Noi**	**Parl-a-vamo** *(Noh-ee paar-laa-vaa-moh)*	We were speaking
(2nd plur.) **Voi**	**Parl-a-vate** *(Voh-ee paar-laa-vaa-teh)*	You were speaking
(3rd plur.) **Loro**	**Parl-a-vano** *(Loh-roh paar-laa-vaa-noh)*	They were speaking

2ND CONJUGATION GROUP (-ERE)

Leggere

Person	Conjugation	Translation
(1st sin.) **Io**	**Legg-e-vo** *(Eeoh ledj-djeh-voh)*	I was reading / used to read
(2nd sin.) **Tu**	**Legg-e-vi** *(Too ledj-djeh-vee)*	You were reading
(3rd sin.) **Lui/Lei**	**Legg-e-va** *(Looee/Leh-ee ledj-djeh-vah)*	She/He/It was reading
(1st plur.) **Noi**	**Legg-e-vamo** *(Noh-ee ledj-djeh-vaa-moh)*	We were reading
(2nd plur.) **Voi**	**Legg-e-vate** *(Voh-ee ledj-djeh-vaa-teh)*	You were reading
(3rd plur.) **Loro**	**Legg-e-vano** *(Loh-roh ledj-djeh-vaa-noh)*	They were reading

We underlined the parts that differ from the first-conjugation rules.

3RD CONJUGATION GROUP (-IRE)

Sentire

Person	Conjugation	Translation
(1st sin.) **Io**	**Sent-i-vo** *(Eeoh sehn-tee-voh)*	I was hearing / used to hear
(2nd sin.) **Tu**	**Sent-i-vi** *(Too sehn-tee-vee)*	You were hearing

(3rd sin.) **Lui/Lei**	**Sent-i̱-va** *(Looee/Leh-ee sehn-tee-vah)*	She/He/It was hearing
(1st plur.) **Noi**	**Sent-i̱-vamo** *(Noh-ee sehn-tee-vaa-moh)*	We were hearing
(2nd plur.) **Voi**	**Sent-i̱-vate** *(Voh-ee sehn-tee-vaa-teh)*	You were hearing
(3rd plur.) **Loro**	**Sent-i̱-vano** *(Loh-roh sehn-tee-vaa-noh)*	They were hearing

We underlined the parts that differ from the first-conjugation rules.

Irregular Verbs

All the irregular verbs in our selected group, with the only exceptions of *fare* and *dire*, follow regular conjugation rules in the *imperfetto* tense. In particular:

Andare

(1st conjugation group) → *And+a+(vo, vi, va, vamo, vate, vano)*.

Stare

(1st conjugation group) → *St+a+(vo, vi, va, vamo, vate, vano)*.

Dovere

(2nd conjugation group) → *Dov+e+(vo, vi, va, vamo, vate, vano)*.

Potere

(2nd conjugation group) → *Pot+e+(vo, vi, va, vamo, vate, vano)*.

Volere

(2nd conjugation group) → *Vol+e+(vo, vi, va, vamo, vate, vano)*.

Sapere

(2nd conjugation group) → *Sap+e+(vo, vi, va, vamo, vate, vano)*.

Venire

(3rd conjugation group) → *Ven+i+(vo, vi, va, vamo, vate, vano)*.

Fare

Person	Conjugation	Translation
(1st sin.) **Io**	**Fac-e-vo** *(Eeoh phaa-tcheh-voh)*	I was doing / used to do
(2nd sin.) **Tu**	**Fac-e-vi** *(Too phaa-tcheh-vee)*	You were doing
(3rd sin.) **Lui/Lei**	**Fac-e-va** *(Looee/Leh-ee phaa-tcheh-vah)*	She/He/It was doing
(1st plur.) **Noi**	**Fac-e-vamo** *(Noh-ee phaa-tcheh-vaa-moh)*	We were doing
(2nd plur.) **Voi**	**Fac-e-vate** *(Voh-ee phaa-tcheh-vaa-teh)*	You were doing
(3rd plur.) **Loro**	**Fac-e-vano** *(Loh-roh phaa-tcheh-vaa-noh)*	They were doing

In this tense, *fare* acts like a regular verb of the 2nd conjugation group (*fare* belongs to the 1st group), with *fac-* as a root word - this happens because, etymologically, the ancestor of *fare* was *facere*. (This also happens in other tenses)

Dire

Person	Conjugation	Translation
(1st sin.) **Io**	**Dic-e-vo** (Eeoh dee-tcheh-voh)	I was saying / used to do say
(2nd sin.) **Tu**	**Dic-e-vi** (Too dee-tcheh-vee)	You were saying
(3rd sin.) **Lui/Lei**	**Dic-e-va** (Looee/Leh-ee dee-tcheh-vah)	She/He/It was saying
(1st plur.) **Noi**	**Dic-e-vamo** (Noh-ee dee-tcheh-vaa-moh)	We were saying
(2nd plur.) **Voi**	**Dic-e-vate** (Voh-ee dee-tcheh-vaa-teh)	You were saying
(3rd plur.) **Loro**	**Dic-e-vano** (Loh-roh dee-tcheh-vaa-noh)	They were saying

In this tense, *dire* acts like a regular verb of the 2nd conjugation group (*dire* belongs to the 3rd group), with *dic-* as a root word - this happens because, etymologically, the ancestor of *dire* was *dicere*. (This also happens in other tenses)

Exercises

1. Complete the following sentences using the verb in brackets in the *imperfetto* tense:

Quando ero piccolo, (giocare = to play)_____ a tennis.

Quando Lucia era piccola, (cantare = to sing)_____ in un coro. (= a choir)

Quando tu eri piccolo, (parlare)_____ raramente (rarely).

Quando voi eravate piccoli, (giocare = to play)_____ sempre insieme (= together)

Quando eravamo piccoli, (amare) _____ la Nutella.

Quando Lucia e Marco erano piccoli, (dire)_____ che si (amare)_____.

2. Complete the following sentences using a verb in the *imperfetto* tense AND the correct preposition (when necessary) AND/OR article:

A: Cosa (fare)_____ (tu)?   B: (parlare)_____ telefono.

Da bambino (avere)_____ cane; Il suo nome _____ Molly.

A: (volere)_____ andare alla festa?

B: Sì, (pensare)_____ di andare.

Sono andato a casa perché non (stare)_____ tanto bene.

Scusa, puoi ripetere per favore?* (essere)_____ distratto. (= distracted)

Quando ci hai chiamati (essere)_____ giardino.

*Common expression for "sorry, can you repeat/say that again please?"

3. Translate the following sentences into English:

Ho comprato un nuovo libro; lo volevo leggere.

_____

Sei stato in Australia? Io ci volevo andare, ma non ho potuto.

_____

Sono tornato (= to come back) a casa prima (=sooner) dal lavoro (= work) perché mi sentivo male.

Questa strada (=street) non era diversa (= different)?

Ho mangiato la torta perché non avevo altro (=else) da mangiare.

Ho sentito un suono strano (= strange). Veniva dalla tua casa.

4. Translate the following sentences into Italian:

I used to play basketball when I was little.

I bought a new phone because the old one wasn't working (funzionare) anymore (più)

She used to love spaghetti. (tip: countable in Italian)

I don't eat pizza anymore, but I used to (eat it).

I wasn't listening (= ascoltare), can you repeat please?

Answer Keys

1. giocavo; cantava: parlavi: giocavate: amavamo; dicevano, amavano

2. facevi, Parlavo al; avevo un, era; Volevi, pensavo; stavo; ero; eravamo in

3. I bought a new book; I wanted to read it. - Have you been to Australia? I wanted to go, but I couldn't. - I came back sooner from work because I was feeling sick. - Didn't this street use to be different? OR Wasn't this street different? - I ate the cake because I didn't have (anything) else to eat. - I heard a strange sound. It was coming/came from your house.

4. (Io) Giocavo a basket/basketball/pallacanestro quando ero piccolo/a. - (io) Ho comprato un nuovo telefono/telefono nuovo perché quello vecchio non funzionava più. - (Lei) amava gli spaghetti. - Non mangio più la pizza, ma la mangiavo. - Non ascoltavo, puoi ripetere per favore?

18. Indicativo Futuro

Indicativo futuro is very similar to the English future simple, and they perfectly match in most uses. Generally speaking, *futuro* is used to describe events that will take place in the future (or in a time that is future to the currently considered time).

However, there are a few specific uses of this future tense that are not present in the English language; only one of these uses is important for us (because it's particularly common), and it is using the future to make a guess or to estimate something.

A: Che ore sono?

A: What's the time?

B: Saranno le quattro.

B: I think it's around four (AM or PM).

A: Quanto sarà alto Marco?

A: How tall do you think is Marco?

B: Sarà alto un metro e ottanta.

B: I think he's one meter and eighty (cm).

A: Chi è quello nella foto?

A: Who's that (guy) in the photo?

B: Boh*, sarà Luca, no**?

B: I don't know, I think it's Luca, am I wrong?

* *Boh* is a common interjection that means " I don't know" and, depending on the situation, it might also mean "I have no clue" or "I don't care to know".

OK, let's see how verbs are conjugated in this tense.

Essere and Avere

<u>Essere</u>

Person	Conjugation	Translation
(1st sin.) **Io**	**Sa**-rò *(Eeoh saa-ròh)*	I will be

(2nd sin.) **Tu**	<u>Sa</u>-rai *(Too saa-raaee)*	You will be
(3rd sin.) **Lui/Lei**	<u>Sa</u>-rà *(Looee/Leh-ee saa-ràh)*	She/He/It will be
(1st plur.) **Noi**	<u>Sa</u>-remo *(Noh-ee saa-reh-moh)*	We will be
(2nd plur.) **Voi**	<u>Sa</u>-rete *(Voh-ee saa-reh-teh)*	You will be
(3rd plur.) **Loro**	<u>Sa</u>-ranno *(Loh-roh saa-raan-noh)*	They will be

The parts that are not underlined are the same as in (all) regular conjugations.

Avere

Person	Conjugation	Translation
(1st sin.) **Io**	<u>Av</u>-rò *(Eeoh aav-ròh)*	I will have
(2nd sin.) **Tu**	<u>Av</u>-rai *(Too aav-raaee)*	You will have
(3rd sin.) **Lui/Lei**	<u>Av</u>-rà *(Looee/Leh-ee aav-ràh)*	She/He/It will have
(1st plur.) **Noi**	<u>Av</u>-remo *(Noh-ee aav-reh-moh)*	We will have
(2nd plur.) **Voi**	<u>Av</u>-rete *(Voh-ee aav-reh-teh)*	You will have
(3rd plur.) **Loro**	<u>Av</u>-ranno *(Loh-roh aav-raan-noh)*	They will have

Regular Verbs

1ST CONJUGATION GROUP (-ARE)
Parlare

Person	Conjugation	Translation
(1st sin.) **Io**	**Parl-e-rò** *(Eeoh paar-leh-ròh)*	I will speak
(2nd sin.) **Tu**	**Parl-e-rai** *(Too paar-leh-raaee)*	You will speak
(3rd sin.) **Lui/Lei**	**Parl-e-rà** *(Looee/Leh-ee paar-leh-ràh)*	She/He/It will speak
(1st plur.) **Noi**	**Parl-e-remo** *(Noh-ee paar-leh-reh-moh)*	We will speak
(2nd plur.) **Voi**	**Parl-e-rete** *(Voh-ee paar-leh-reh-teh)*	You will speak
(3rd plur.) **Loro**	**Parl-e-ranno** *(Loh-roh paar-leh-raan-noh)*	They will speak

2ND CONJUGATION GROUP (-ERE)
Leggere

Person	Conjugation	Translation
(1st sin.) **Io**	**Legg-e-rò** *(Eeoh ledj-djeh-ròh)*	I will read
(2nd sin.) **Tu**	**Legg-e-rai** *(Too ledj-djeh-raaee)*	You will read

(3rd sin.) **Lui/Lei**	**Legg-e-rà** *(Looee/Leh-ee ledj-djeh-ràh)*	She/He/It will read
(1st plur.) **Noi**	**Legg-e-remo** *(Noh-ee ledj-djeh-reh-moh)*	We will read
(2nd plur.) **Voi**	**Legg-e-rete** *(Voh-ee ledj-djeh-reh-teh)*	You will read
(3rd plur.) **Loro**	**Legg-e-ranno** *(Loh-roh ledj-djeh-raan-noh)*	They will read

The rules for the 2nd group are the same that are used for the 1st conjugation group, in this tense.

3RD CONJUGATION GROUP (-IRE)

Sentire

Person	Conjugation	Translation
(1st sin.) **Io**	**Sent-i-rò** *(Eeoh sehn-tee-ròh)*	I will hear
(2nd sin.) **Tu**	**Sent-i-rai** *(Too sehn-tee-raaee)*	You will hear
(3rd sin.) **Lui/Lei**	**Sent-i-rà** *(Looee/Leh-ee sehn-tee-ràh)*	She/He/It will hear
(1st plur.) **Noi**	**Sent-i-remo** *(Noh-ee sehn-tee-reh-moh)*	We will hear
(2nd plur.) **Voi**	**Sent-i-rete** *(Voh-ee sehn-tee-reh-teh)*	You will hear

(3rd plur.) **Loro**	**Sent-i-ranno** (Loh-roh sehn-tee-raan-noh)	They will hear

We underlined the parts that differ from the rules for the 1st and 2nd conjugations.

Irregular Verbs

<u>Andare</u>

Person	Conjugation	Translation
(1st sin.) **Io**	**And-rò** (Eeoh aand-ròh)	I will go
(2nd sin.) **Tu**	**And-rai** (Too aand-raaee)	You will go
(3rd sin.) **Lui/Lei**	**And-rà** (Looee/Leh-ee aand-ràh)	She/He/It will go
(1st plur.) **Noi**	**And-remo** (Noh-ee aand-reh-moh)	We will go
(2nd plur.) **Voi**	**And-rete** (Voh-ee aand-reh-teh)	You will go
(3rd plur.) **Loro**	**And-ranno** (Loh-roh aand-raan-noh)	They will go

The only irregularity is the absence of the central -e- before the suffix.

Fare

Person	Conjugation	Translation
(1st sin.) **Io**	**Fa-rò** *(Eeoh phaa-ròh)*	I will do
(2nd sin.) **Tu**	**Fa-rai** *(Too phaa-raaee)*	You will do
(3rd sin.) **Lui/Lei**	**Fa-rà** *(Looee/Leh-ee phaa-ràh)*	She/He/It will do
(1st plur.) **Noi**	**Fa-remo** *(Noh-ee phaa-reh-moh)*	We will do
(2nd plur.) **Voi**	**Fa-rete** *(Voh-ee phaa-reh-teh)*	You will do
(3rd plur.) **Loro**	**Fa-ranno** *(Loh-roh phaa-raan-noh)*	They will do

The root word is irregular, and so is the absence of the central -e- before the suffix.

Stare

Person	Conjugation	Translation
(1st sin.) **Io**	**Sta-rò** *(Eeoh staa-ròh)*	I will be physically
(2nd sin.) **Tu**	**Sta-rai** *(Too staa-raaee)*	You will be physically
(3rd sin.) **Lui/Lei**	**Sta-rà** *(Looee/Leh-ee staa-ràh)*	She/He/It will be physically

Person	Conjugation	Translation
(1st plur.) **Noi**	**Sta-remo** *(Noh-ee staa-reh-moh)*	We will be physically
(2nd plur.) **Voi**	**Sta-rete** *(Voh-ee staa-reh-teh)*	You will be physically
(3rd plur.) **Loro**	**Sta-ranno** *(Loh-roh staa-raan-noh)*	They will be physically

The root word is irregular, and so is the absence of the central -e- before the suffix.

Dovere

Person	Conjugation	Translation
(1st sin.) **Io**	**Dov-rò** *(Eeoh dohv-ròh)*	I will have to
(2nd sin.) **Tu**	**Dov-rai** *(Too dohv-raaee)*	You will have to
(3rd sin.) **Lui/Lei**	**Dov-rà** *(Looee/Leh-ee dohv-ràh)*	She/He/It will have to
(1st plur.) **Noi**	**Dov-remo** *(Noh-ee dohv-reh-moh)*	We will have to
(2nd plur.) **Voi**	**Dov-rete** *(Voh-ee dohv-reh-teh)*	You will have to
(3rd plur.) **Loro**	**Dov-ranno** *(Loh-roh dohv-raan-noh)*	They will have to

The only irregularity is the absence of the central -e- before the suffix.

Potere

Person	Conjugation	Translation
(1st sin.) **Io**	**Pot-rò** (*Eeoh poht-ròh*)	I will be able to
(2nd sin.) **Tu**	**Pot-rai** (*Too poht-raaee*)	You will be able to
(3rd sin.) **Lui/Lei**	**Pot-rà** (*Looee/Leh-ee poht-ràh*)	She/He/It will be able to
(1st plur.) **Noi**	**Pot-remo** (*Noh-ee poht-reh-moh*)	We will be able to
(2nd plur.) **Voi**	**Pot-rete** (*Voh-ee poht-reh-teh*)	You will be able to
(3rd plur.) **Loro**	**Pot-ranno** (*Loh-roh poht-raan-noh*)	They will be able to

The only irregularity is the absence of the central -e- before the suffix.

Volere

Person	Conjugation	Translation
(1st sin.) **Io**	**Vor-rò** (*Eeoh vohr-ròh*)	I will want
(2nd sin.) **Tu**	**Vor-rai** (*Too vohr-raaee*)	You will want
(3rd sin.) **Lui/Lei**	**Vor-rà** (*Looee/Leh-ee vohr-ràh*)	She/He/It will want
(1st plur.) **Noi**	**Vor-remo** (*Noh-ee vohr-reh-moh*)	We will want

| (2nd plur.) Voi | **Vor-rete** *(Voh-ee vohr-reh-teh)* | You will want |
| (3rd plur.) **Loro** | **Vor-ranno** *(Loh-roh vohr-raan-noh)* | They will want |

The root word is irregular, and so is the absence of the central -e- before the suffix.

Sapere

Person	Conjugation	Translation
(1st sin.) **Io**	**Sap-rò** *(Eeoh saap-ròh)*	I will know
(2nd sin.) **Tu**	**Sap-rai** *(Too saap-raaee)*	You will know
(3rd sin.) **Lui/Lei**	**Sap-rà** *(Looee/Leh-ee saap-ràh)*	She/He/It will know
(1st plur.) **Noi**	**Sap-remo** *(Noh-ee saap-reh-moh)*	We will know
(2nd plur.) **Voi**	**Sap-rete** *(Voh-ee saap-reh-teh)*	You will know
(3rd plur.) **Loro**	**Sap-ranno** *(Loh-roh saap-raan-noh)*	They will know

The only irregularity is the absence of the central -e- before the suffix.

Venire

Person	Conjugation	Translation
(1st sin.) **Io**	**Ver-rò** (*Eeoh vehr-ròh*)	I will come
(2nd sin.) **Tu**	**Ver-rai** (*Too vehr-raaee*)	You will come
(3rd sin.) **Lui/Lei**	**Ver-rà** (*Looee/Leh-ee vehr-ràh*)	She/He/It will come
(1st plur.) **Noi**	**Ver-remo** (*Noh-ee vehr-reh-moh*)	We will come
(2nd plur.) **Voi**	**Ver-rete** (*Voh-ee vehr-reh-teh*)	You will come
(3rd plur.) **Loro**	**Ver-ranno** (*Loh-roh vehr-raan-noh*)	They will come

The root word is irregular, and so is the absence of the central -i- before the suffix.

Dire

Person	Conjugation	Translation
(1st sin.) **Io**	**Di-rò** (*Eeoh dee-ròh*)	I will say
(2nd sin.) **Tu**	**Di-rai** (*Too dee-raaee*)	You will say
(3rd sin.) **Lui/Lei**	**Di-rà** (*Looee/Leh-ee dee-ràh*)	She/He/It will say
(1st plur.) **Noi**	**Di-remo** (*Noh-ee dee-reh-moh*)	We will say

(2nd plur.) **Voi**	**Di-rete** *(Voh-ee dee-reh-teh)*	You will say
(3rd plur.) **Loro**	**Di-ranno** *(Loh-roh dee-raan-noh)*	They will say

The root word is irregular, and so is the absence of the central -i- before the suffix.

Exercises

1. Complete the following sentences with the correct form of either *essere* or *avere*, in the future (indicativo futuro).

Io _____ un dottore. (= a doctor)

Luca _____ a Londra. (= London)

Luca e Paolo _____ via.

Loro _____ una bella casa.

Tu _____ paura. (= fear)

Voi _____ eroi.

2. Complete the following sentences with the correct form of the verb in brackets, in the future tense (indicativo futuro).

(venire) Noi _____ dall'Italia.

(fare) Tu mi _____ ridere.

(stare) Io e Paolo _____ bene.

(sapere) Lucia _____.

(potere) Io _____ andare.

(volere) Tue e Luca _____ il gelato?

3. Complete the following sentences with the correct form of the verb in brackets, in the future tense (indicativo futuro).

(andare) Noi _____ a Parigi.

(fare) Loro _____ i pancake.

(stare) Io e Paolo _____ a Roma.

(dovere) Lucia _____ andare.

(leggere) Io _____ un libro.

(venire) Tu e Luca _____ alla festa?

4. Translate the following sentences into English:

Ho comprato un biglietto (ticket) per l'Italia, ma non penso (to think) andrò.
_____

Penso farò come hai detto.
_____

Quanto costerà un biglietto per gli Stati Uniti?
_____

Il museo (museum) chiuderà (close) alle 20.
_____

5. Translate the following sentences into Italian:

The dog ran away (scappare*), but he'll be back (tornare).
_____

My friends Marta and Lucia will be in (a) Rome next (prossimo) weekend.
_____

I will tell you, there (ci) will be a problem.
_____

What I did and what I will do are my personal (personale) choices (scelta)

*this is a verb of movement

Answer Keys

1. sarò, sarà, saranno, avranno, avrai, sarete

2. verremo, farai, staremo, saprà, potrò, vorrete

3. andremo, faranno, staremo, dovrà, leggerò, verrete

4. I bought a ticket to Italy, but I don't think I'll go. - I think I'll do like you said. - How much <u>do you think</u> - OR - <u>can</u> a ticket to the United States cost? - The museum will close at 8 PM.

5. Il cane è scappato, ma (lui) tornerà. - Le mie amiche Marta e Lucia saranno a Roma il prossimo weekend. - Ti dirò, ci sarà un problema. - Cosa ho fatto e cosa farò sono mie scelte personali. OR Quello/ciò che ho fatto e quello/ciò che farò sono scelte mie personali.

Verbs Conjugation 3

Congratulations for making it this far! These final two lessons will cover two smaller topics that are quick to go through, but will come very handy.

In particular, we're going to discuss two moods, *infinito* and *participio*, which both have 2 only tenses: present and past. Quick and easy.

These tenses correspond to the infinitive and participle tenses in English and are used in a similar way. Let's see what they look like in Italian!

19. Modo Infinito

Modo infinito, the infinitive mood, is an indefinite mood (there are no 1st, 2nd or 3rd person, singular or plural) that only exists in a present or past tense. The use is basically the same as in English, which is why we won't have specific exercises for this lesson (it would end up in a pointless "name the verb" game).

The only relevant difference is that in the Italian language, since it doesn't have a present or past continuous, you can use infinito when it's about setting a condition or specifying something. For example:

Essere quì è un grande onore → To be here is a great honor → Being here is a great honor.

Essere stato in carcere non aiuta C To have been in jail doesn't help → Having been (spent time) in jail doesn't help

As these are very simple conjugations with very little irregularities, we will just mention the conjugations for *essere* and *avere*, and the general rule for all other verbs.

Before doing that, we need to mention one last thing: all Italian verbs, in the present infinitive, can drop the final "E". This happens quite frequently when talking fast, in poetry, and whenever it just sounds better to do so. It is not a rule, and both forms are always correct.

Parlare → Parlar ; Leggere → Legger ; Sentire → Sentir

This is especially frequent with the auxiliary *essere* and *avere,* when they're used at the infinitive in composite verbs (namely the *infinito passato* of other verbs):

Avere parlato → Aver parlato ; Avere letto → Aver letto ; Avere sentito → Aver sentito

Essere and Avere

Let's see how these verbs are conjugated in the present tense:

Essere

Infinito presente	**Infinito passato**
Essere	Essere stato,a,i,e
Translation	
To be	To have been / having been

Avere

Infinito presente	**Infinito passato**
Avere	Avere avuto
Translation	

| To have | To have had / having had |

Other Verbs

Regular and irregular verbs are all "regular" in forming the present infinitive. As for the past infinitive, there can be two issues:

- You have to choose the correct auxiliary verb (*essere* or *avere*) for both regular and irregular verbs.
- Some verbs might have an irregular past participle, which is needed for this composite tense.

In fact, the infinito passato tense consists of a *verbo servile*, in the infinitive tense, plus the *participio passato* of that verb. We will not anticipate how regular verbs are conjugated in this tense, as it will be the topic of our next lesson.

20. Modo Participio

Participio mood consists in 2 tenses, *presente* and *passato*, with 2 very different uses. *Participio presente* is used mostly as a noun, and identifies the doer of the action, while *participio passato* is mostly used as an adjective, or to construct composite verbal forms.

Some examples of present participle can be:

Comprante, from comprare = to buy, → buyer

Amante, from amare = to love, → lover

And some examples of past participle can be

Comprato → Bought

Amato → Loved

As simple as this. Let's now look at how verbs get conjugated in these tenses. Consider that many regular verbs have an irregular *participio passato*, especially verbs in the 2nd conjugation. *Leggere* (to read) is one of these verbs, so we'll also use the conjugation of the verb *credere* (to believe) to show you a regular formation of the past participle for the 2nd group.

Essere and Avere

Essere

Participio presente	Participio passato
Essente, i	Stato,a,i,e
Translation	
Be-er (He who's being)	Been

Avere

Participio presente	Participio passato
Avente, i	Avuto,a,i,e
Translation	
Have-er (He who's having)	Had

Regular Verbs

1ST CONJUGATION GROUP (-ARE)

Parlare

Participio presente	Participio passato
Parl-a-nte, i	Parl-a-to,a,i,e
Translation	
Talker (He who's talking)	Talked

2ND CONJUGATION GROUP (-ERE)

Credere

Participio presente	Participio passato
Legg-<u>e</u>-nte, i	Cred-<u>u</u>-to,a,i,e
Translation	
Believer (He who's believing)	Believed

We underlined the parts that differ from the first-conjugation rules.

Leggere

Participio presente	Participio passato
Legg-<u>e</u>-nte, i	Letto,a,i,e (irregular!)
Translation	

| Reader (He who's reading) | Read |

3RD CONJUGATION GROUP (-IRE)
Sentire

Participio presente	Participio passato
Sent-e-nte, i OR Senziente, i (irregular)	Sent-i-to,a,i,e
Translation	
Hearer (He who's hearing)	Heard

We underlined the parts that differ from the first-conjugation rules. *Participio presente* follows the same rules that are used for the 2nd conjugation group.

Irregular Verbs

Finally, our chosen group of irregular verbs:

Andare forms regular participles: *andante* and *andato*

Fare

Participio presente	Participio passato
Fac-e-nte, i	Fatto,a,i,e
Translation	
Doer (He who's reading)	Done

We underlined the parts that differ from the conjugation of regular verbs from this group.

<u>Stare</u> forms regular participles: *stante* and *stato*

<u>Dovere</u> forms regular participles: *dovente* and *dovuto*

<u>Potere</u> forms regular participles: *potente* and *potuto*

<u>Volere</u> forms regular participles: *volente* and *voluto*

<u>Sapere</u>

Participio presente	Participio passato
Sap-<u>i</u>-e-nte, i	Sap-uto,a,i,e
Translation	
Kower (He who's knowing)	Known

We underlined the parts that differ from the conjugation of regular verbs from this group.

<u>Venire</u>

Participio presente	Participio passato
Ven-<u>i</u>-e-nte, i	Ven-uto,a,i,e
Translation	
Comer (He who's coming)	Come

We underlined the parts that differ from the conjugation of regular verbs from this group

Dire

Participio presente	Participio passato
Dic-e-nte, i	Detto,a,i,e
Translation	
Sayer (He who's saying)	Said

We underlined the parts that differ from the conjugation of regular verbs from this group

In addition, there are a number of verbs, which are otherwise regular, that form irregular past participles. This can happen frequently, because verbs in the *participio* mood can also have separate uses, other than the verbal function. This means that, in time, they have undergone a separate "evolutionary push", when used as a noun or adjective.

Here's a list of common verbs that are regular, for the most part, but form irregular past participles:

Translation	Verb	Past participle
To turn on	Accendere	Acceso,a,i,e
To open	Aprire	Aperto,a,i,e
To ask	Chiedere	Chiesto,a,i,e
To know	Conoscere	Conosciuto,a,i,e
To convince	Convincere	Convinto,a,i,e
To run	Correre	Corso,a,i,e

To grow	Crescere	Cresciuto,a,i,e
To include	Includere	Incluso,a,i,e
To read	Leggere	Letto,a,i,e
To put	Mettere	Messo,a,i,e
To move	Muovere	Mosso,a,i,e
To be born	Nascere	Nato,a,i,e
To hide	Nascondere	Nascosto,a,i,e
To offer	Offrire	Offerto,a,i,e
To lose	Perdere	Perso,a,i,e OR Perduto,a,i,e
To take or To get	Prendere	Preso,a,i,e
To discover or To uncover	Scoprire	Scoperto,a,i,e
To translate	Tradurre	Tradotto,a,i,e
To kill	Uccidere	Ucciso,a,i,e
To win	Vincere	Vinto,a,i,e

A smaller number of verbs have an irregular participio presente, but we are not going to mention these because this tense is rather uncommon (whereas participio passato is used for all the composite forms of other mood's tenses).

The one example that is worth knowing for now is *studiare*, that is *studente,i* (he who's studying) in the present participle. *Studente* is also the noun for student, and it has its feminine version in *studentessa*.

Last but not least, let's discuss gender and number. Both *participio* tenses can vary in gender and number (although the two genders form identical words for *participio presente*), but when do we need to do it?

Whenever these words are used as a noun or adjective, they need to be in the correct gender and number. When they're used as verbs, it depends. *Participio presente* is only used in rather technical constructions, and it normally does not vary.

Participio passato always needs to agree in number and gender with the subject of the sentence when it's used in composite verbs that have *essere* as an auxiliary verb. When the auxiliary verb is *avere* it normally does not vary, but it might need to vary in some cases, in order to agree in gender and number with the direct object. This is especially common when the direct object is in the form of a pronominal particle, for example:

Ho comprato la penna. - I bought the pen.

OR

Ho comprato quella. - I bought that one.

Ho comprato lei/essa. - I bought it

BUT

L'ho comprata. (la ho comprat<u>a</u>) - I bought it.

Exercises

1. Complete the following sentences using the *participio presente* of the verbs in brackets:

È meglio chiedere ai ____sapienti____ (sapere). [It's better/best to ask the learned ones (lit. knowing ones)]

La voce _____ (narrare) è James Earl Jones. [The narrating voice is James Earl Jones]

Il grillo _____ (parlare) è l'amico di Pinocchio. [The talking cricket is Pinocchio's friend]

Questa zuppa è _____ (eccellere). [This soup is excellent.]

Lo _____ (studiare) ha molto da imparare, ma anche l'_____ (insegnare). [The student has a lot to learn, but (so does) the teacher too.]

2. Complete the following sentences using the *participio passato* of the verbs in brackets:

Ho _____ (scoprire) un giardino _____ (nascondere). [I discovered a hidden garden]

Ha _____ (dire) quello che ha _____ (sentire) . [He/She said what he/she heard]

L'offerta _____ (includere) nel prezzo è ottima. [The offer included in the the price is great (The offer is great for this price)]

_____ (convincere) di questo, Maria ha _____ (sbagliare = to make a mistake). [Convinced of this, Maria made a mistake]

3. Translate the following sentences into English:

Essere un soldato (soldier) è un grande onore.

_____

Essere stato un poliziotto mi ha cambiato la vita.

_____

Ho male alle gambe (legs) per aver corso troppo.

_____

Sono fortunato (lucky) a essere vivo.

_____

4. Translate the following sentences into Italian:

Wearing (portare) this medal (medaglia) is an honor.
___

Don't talk too much, actions (azione) are better than a thousand words.
___

To be or not to be, this is the question. ("question" is historically translated with *il dilemma*)
___

I've always wanted to go to space (spazio).
___

I finished (finire) the last line (riga) of the last exercise in this book.
___

Answer Keys

1. narrante; parlante; eccellente; studente, insegnante

2. scoperto, nascosto; detto, sentito; inclusa; convinta, sbagliato

3. Being a soldier is a great honor. - Having been a policeman changed my life. - I have pain in (my) legs [my legs hurt] for having run too much (for running too much). - I'm lucky to be alive.

4. Portare questa medaglia è un onore. - Non parlare troppo, le azioni sono meglio di mille parole. - Essere o non essere, questo è il dilemma. - Ho sempre voluto andare nello spazio. - Ho finito l'ultima riga dell'ultimo esercizio in questo libro.

Conclusion

"The limits of my language mean the limits of my world."

- Ludwig Wittgenstein

Congratulazioni! *Hai finito il tuo primo libro di grammatica italiana!* I know, it was a long and difficult voyage, but look at all the progress you made!

You're now able to understand virtually any simple Italian sentence in the present, in the future, and in most past constructions. Since you learned the language from its basis, vocabulary is your only limit now.

In this final part of the book, we'll talk about the next steps to take to keep improving in Italian. First, we'll see how you can keep working on the things you already learned, in order to strengthen your current knowledge and further investigate smaller aspects of the language.

Then, we'll give you some advice on what we believe is the best way to keep on learning Italian. In particular, we'll talk about what topics are best for you to take up next and what methods of study could bring the best results.

A: How to consolidate your new knowledge

Right now, you have built great language skills that let you understand most sentences in Italian. Your current main problems are 2:

- Vocabulary
- Common expressions with a peculiar grammar (Idioms, specific use of prepositions, colloquial expressions)

Both these topics can be considered part of the practical use of the language, which is the area where you can make the most progress now.

In order to consolidate your current knowledge, you should consider the various kinds of practical approach to the language, most of which we already mentioned throughout the book (our Phrasebook, our Collection of Stories, movies, podcasts, tv shows, language-exchange apps etc.).

Secondarily, you can keep practicing on the grammar topics we learned together. Your options include the numerous exercises on our Phrasebook for Adult Beginners, re-doing the exercises in this book with verbs, adjectives or prepositions of your choice, or turning to a new workbook from a different author or an online website with A1-A2 grammar exercises.

A third option could be using an app. There are many apps out there that can help you consolidate your current knowledge, either language apps or language-exchange apps; most of them are free, or at least they let you use the main features without a premium account.

If you struggled with some specific topics throughout this book, you should then try and target these topics specifically. Online you can find very good explanations of all the single grammar topics; there are various reliable websites that present the topic with different examples and visual material. Maybe hearing it from a different voice will do the trick. Otherwise, you can choose to turn to YouTube, where you can find many excellent bilingual teachers.

Most of these YouTubers offer videos on various grammar topics, with practical applications and useful insights. We did not mention the possibility to join an Italian class or to hire an Italian teacher, as they're clearly among the best options, time and budget permitting.

B: Next steps to keep learning Italian

Let's now discuss what you should do next to become more proficient in Italian. On the grammar side, there are still some tenses and moods for you to learn; other than that, it's mostly articulated constructions, specific cases and exceptions (advanced Italian grammar consists of these topics).

In particular, you should learn how to use *verbi riflessivi* and the verb *piacere*; after that, you should learn about *congiuntivo, futuro anteriore* and *condizionale*, before all the remaining tenses and moods. Then you should get to know about *verbi pronominali, verbi impersonali* and a couple more specific cases.

Beside verbs, you should learn how to modify nouns (yes, a noun can be further modified, it's not just gender and number) and some specific uses of adjectives and adverbs.

Most of these topics, except for the ones that are too advanced, will be the focus of our Intermediate-Level Grammar Workbook. We designed our intermediate-level book to be complementary to this beginner-level book. This means that, if you keep trusting us for your future studies, you can make sure to avoid skipping any topic or studying the same topic twice.

As you progress, it will be more and more important to also target your listening and speaking skills, as well as practice your reading skills on different types of texts, such as novels, essays or articles. On our side, we'll do our best to keep offering you useful material that can support you in your learning venture.

The more you progress, however, the more it is important to differentiate your sources and expose yourself to various uses of the Italian language. For this reason, at some point you will have to stop relying on books only, if that's been the case.

This is all for now! We hope you enjoyed learning with us, and we wish you all the best. See you in the Intermediate-Level Workbook, sempre che ti sia piaciuto studiare con noi e che tu abbia ancora intenzione di navigare i meandri della grammatica Italiana, oltre che arrivare ad un livello che ti renda in grado di tradurre interamente questa frase, senza Google Translate!

$29 FREE BONUSES

Italian Verbs Cheatsheets
Master Italian Verbs Today!

Scan QR code above to claim your free bonuses!

―――――― OR ――――――

visit exploretowin.com/italianbonuses

Ready to Sound Like an Italian Native?

Inside these 3 adult beginner-friendly Italian verbs cheatsheets, you'll find:

- ✓ Practical tenses for the most common Italian vocabulary
- ✓ Charts to help you master the conjugation of common Italian verbs
- ✓ Exercises to help you practice conjugating verbs in any tense

Scan QR code above to claim your free bonuses!

―――――― OR ――――――

visit exploretowin.com/italianbonuses

Made in United States
North Haven, CT
27 November 2022

27192184R00145